The Book of Be

The Book of
BEATLE LISTS

Bill Harry

JAVELIN BOOKS
POOLE · DORSET

First published in the UK 1985 by Javelin Books,
Link House, West Street, Poole, Dorset, BH 115 1LL

Compilation copyright © 1985 Bill Harry

Distributed in the United States by
Sterling Publishing Co., Inc.,
2 Park Avenue, New York, NY 10016

British Library Cataloguing in Publication Data

Harry, Bill
  The book of Beatle lists.
  1. Beatles
  I. Title
  784.5′0092′2   ML421.B4

ISBN 0 7137 1521 9

Typeset by Spire Print Services Ltd,
Salisbury, Wilts.
Printed in Great Britain by Cox and Wyman, Reading.

Contents

Acknowledgements

My thanks to: Stuart Booth and my editor Maggie O' Hanlon for their encouragement; Spartan Records for *The Royal Philharmonic Orchestra Plays the Beatles* and *Off The Beatle Track*; the staff of *Beatles Unlimited*; Roger Akehurst of Beatles Now; Marsha Ewing (and all at Southfork) for Instant Karma; Mike McCartney (who I swore I'd make famous!) for his photograph; Phil Day of United Artists for the 'Caveman' photo; Moira Bellas of WEA Records for the Rutles pic; the Atlantic Tower Hotel, Liverpool; Tony Wadsworth, Kathy Gardner of EMI and the EMI Press Office for the Paul McCartney, Swinging Blue Jeans and Fourmost photographs and album covers for *Sgt. Pepper*, *The Beatles Reel Music* and *Mersey Beat*; Liz and Jim Hughes for permission to reproduce some of their copyright photographs, including the early shot of the Beatles on stage at the Cavern; Ron Smith of Merseyside County Council for permission to reproduce material. Other photographs from the Mersey Beat archives. Thanks also to Helen and Ian Drummond, Steve Phillips. Rosario Grasso, Jacques Volcouve, Joel Glazier and the many other dedicated Beatle fans for their regular help and enthusiasm.

Introduction

The first list in which the Beatles appeared was in the October 1961 issue of *Mersey Beat*. Part of 'The Roving I' column by Bob Wooler, listed his ten most popular local Rock groups.

1　The Beatles
2　Gerry & The Pacemakers
3　Rory Storm & The Hurricanes
4　The Remo Four
5　The Strangers
6　Johnny Sandon & The Searchers
7　Karl Terry and the Cruisers
8　Mark Peters & The Cyclones
9　Ray & The Del Renas
10　The Big Three

Bob added the rider: 'excluding the Bluegenes, of course. They are beyond comparison. They are in a class of their own.'

The Beatles found themselves cropping up in many lists in *Mersey Beat*, for instance the line-up of the Friday 1st December 1961 gig at the Tower Ballroom, New Brighton:

The Beatles
Rory Storm & The Hurricanes
Dale Roberts & The Jaywalkers
Kingsize Taylor & The Dominoes
Derry & The Seniors
Steve Day & The Drifters

In the most important list they topped the list of winners of the *Mersey Beat* poll – twice! They next topped the 'Mersey Charts' with *Love Me Do* and the succeeding lists comprised their amazing achievements all over the world as they became the most successful musical phenomenon of the twentieth century.

This book has been fun to compile and as each new list was included, ideas for further ones emerged. Who knows, I may yet compile a second volume. In the meantime, I hope *The Book of Beatle Lists* will provide you with some hours of pleasure.

Bill Harry, London, March 1984

1 A Taste of Trivia – 1

Most Beatle fans, fully conversant with the group's history, are avid for little-known facts in the saga of the Fab Four. Here is the first selection of fifty items of Beatles' trivia.

1   The Beatles created another 'record' in 1964 when they became the only act to replace themselves at No. 1 in the charts on two occasions. *I Want to Hold Your Hand* was knocked from the top position in the USA by *She Loves You* which, in turn, was replaced at No. 1 by *Can't Buy Me Love*.

2   During their career, the Beatles only worked with four record producers: Bert Kaempfert, Mike Smith, George Martin and Phil Spector.

3   Paul declined an offer from the National Theatre in 1967 to compose music for their interpretation of Shakespeare's *As You Like It*.

4   Elton John is Sean Lennon's godfather.

5   Astrid Kirchnerr, original girl friend of Klaus Voorman, who became engaged to Stuart Sutcliffe, eventually married Gibson Kemp, the drummer who replaced Ringo Starr in Rory Storm & The Hurricanes.

6   Frank Sinatra called George Harrison's *Something* 'The greatest love song of the past fifty years.'

7   The Beatles originally intended calling their seventh British album *Abracadabra*, but the name had already been used by another band, so they setted on *Revolver*.

8   George Harrison's first wife Pattie married his best friend, ace guitarist Eric Clapton.

9   John Lennon originally envisaged a thousand Tibetan monks chanting in the background of *The Void*, a song which underwent a name change to *Tomorrow Never Knows* – and the thousand monks became a makeshift choir of members of London's Speakeasy club.

10   Ringo Starr was elected Vice-President of Leeds University Students' Union in 1964.

11   Linda McCartney's family name was originally Epstein, the same as that of the Beatles' first manager, but her father

Imagine Twiggy and the Beatles starring in *Lord of the Flies*.

changed the name to Eastman. Because she was a photographer, journalists mistakenly believed she was an Eastman/Kodak heiress.

12   The original Cavern stage was cut up into small pieces and sold as 'Beatleboard', with the proceeds donated to the famine relief charity Oxfam.

13   Graham Nash of The Hollies, Keith Moon of the Who, Gary Leeds of the Walker Brothers, Mick Jagger and his girl-friend Marianne Faithfull, Keith Richard of the Rolling Stones and Jane Asher and Pattie Boyd were among the voices raised in the chorus of *All You Need is Love* during the Beatles' appearance on the *Our World* TV special.

14   Ringo once claimed that his ambition as a Beatle was to earn enough money to open a chain of hairdressing salons.

15   The Ladders was the name that John, George and Ringo decided on calling themselves when Paul caused the dissolution of the Beatles' partnership. His replacement on bass was to be Klaus Voorman.

16 The strip of foliage above the flowers on the *Sgt Pepper* sleeve is comprised of marijuana plants.

17 Paul McCartney demonstrated his songwriting ability to movie star Dustin Hoffman by penning a song on a topic suggested by the actor. Hoffman quoted Pablo Picasso's last words and Paul wrote *Picasso's Last Words*.

18 John was only the first of Julia Lennon's four children.

19 Capitol Records rearranged the design of the cover of the *Help!* album in which each member of the group spells out a letter of the title in semaphore, resulting in the American release reading *HPEL*!

20 One of the most unusual of the Beatle's novelty discs was *Frankenstein Meets The Beatles* by Jeckyl & Hyde.

21 The Boyd sisters have both been immortalised in song. Pattie was the inspiration behind Eric Clapton's *Layla* and her sister Jenny inspired Donovan's hit *Jennifer Juniper*.

22 The group's largest live audience in the USA was the 65,000 gathered at New York's Shea Stadium on 15th August 1965.

23 Beatles' relatives who released records included Paul's brother Mike, John's father Freddie, George's sister Louise and Paul's cousin Kate Robbins. Mike and Kate's records were the only ones to make the charts. Julian Lennon became a hit artist with his very first single, *It's Never Too Late*, in October 1984.

24 When the Beatles appeared for a short season at the Paris Olympia in 1964, they requested a meeting with Brigitte Bardot – but she was in Brazil at the time.

25 Former drummer Pete Best revealed that when the group was hard-up in Hamburg, they attempted to mug a sailor.

26 John Lennon referred to *The Beatles* White double album as 'The Son of Sergeant Pepper.'

27 *She Loves You* became the first single to ever top sales of $1\frac{1}{2}$ million copies in the UK.

28 On 24th April 1968, the Beatles' Apple Records turned down the opportunity of signing David Bowie, who was to become one of the biggest solo superstars of rock – a boob almost as big as that of Decca's Dick Rowe turning down the Beatles!

29   John Lennon penned twenty-seven No. 1 hits which was, at one time, more chart-toppers than any other writer. He was overtaken by Paul, who incidentally co-wrote four of John's No. 1s.

30   George Harrison and Derek Taylor once began work on a musical for the stage, based on the Beatles' Apple empire.

31   When in Paris in January 1964, the Beatles recorded at the Pathé Marconi studios – the only time in their career when they made studio recordings outside the UK. Their earlier Hamburg sessions were as a backing band, prior to Ringo joining the quartet.

32   Capitol Records in the USA refused John Lennon's offer to design a cover for the *Rock 'n' Roll Music* album.

33   One of the carefully selected items of twentieth century culture buried in a time capsule in California and due to be opened in the twenty-first century is a copy of the film *A Hard Day's Night*.

34   In 1966, the Beatles showed how they felt about apartheid by refusing to tour South Africa.

35   The Beatles originally wrote *Back In The USSR* for Twiggy. Incidentally, the Cockney model was due to appear with the Beatles in a film of *Lord Of the Rings*, but the project was cancelled.

36   *I Want To Hold Your Hand*, when issued in 1963, was the first record ever to sell a million copies on advance orders.

37   The sleeve notes for the Italian release of the *A Hard Days Night* (*Tutti Per Uno*) album, when translated into English, began: 'Here they are also changed into actors, these four lads from Liverpool who upset England and the world's music business, becoming almost as important and feared as the 'Home Fleet' of Queen Victoria's golden age and quoted in the Stock Exchange similar to the shares of the East India Company.'

38   George Harrison made a guest appearance in the Monty Python film *The Life of Brian* as Mr. Papadopoulis.

39   The original *Beatles Book*, the monthly magazine which was their 'official' voice in the sixties, ran to seventy-seven monthly issues.

40   There is a morse code message on the *Strawberry Fields*

Forever single which spells out the letters 'J' and 'L'.

41   John Lennon bought a supermarket on Hayling Island in Sussex for his old school chum Pete Shotton.

42   Prior to his tragic death and following his departure from the Rolling Stones, Brian Jones had aspirations of joining the Beatles and actually performed on two of their records.

43   When Beatlemania first ran rife in the USA, there were many bizarre items of merchandise – including bottled 'Beatle Breath' on sale in New York.

44   Before the decision was taken to call the first Beatle's film *A Hard Day's Night* (from a suggestion by Ringo about the phrase which appeared in John's book *In His Own Write*), several other names, including *Beatlemania*, were suggested. One name which Paul McCartney came up with was *What Little Old Man?*, obviously referring to the Wilfred Brambell role as John McCartney.

45   *Sgt Pepper's Lonely Hearts Club Band* reached No. 1 in the charts on four separate occasions between 1967 and 1968.

46   The Beatles' initial appearance on *The Ed Sullivan Show* on American TV in 1964 drew an audience of 73,000,000 – the biggest TV audience ever recorded until that time.

47   By January 1984, Paul McCartney had a total of 102 hit records in the USA, including twenty-nine No. 1 records. Despite this, his first No. 1 single as a solo artist, *The Pipes of Peace*, didn't top the charts until January 1984. His previous No. 1s had been collaborations, hits with the Beatles and Wings, plus duets with Linda, Stevie Wonder and Michael Jackson.

48   The Beatles were the only artists to hit the American charts with both an English and foreign language version of the same number. This occurred when their German *Sie Leibt Dich* charted in 1964, following their chart-topping version in English of the same number *She Loves You*.

49   When in Hamburg, the impecunious Beatles used to snip the wires from club pianos for use as guitar strings.

50   In 'Fade Out', the final episode of the cult British Sixties TV series *The Prisoner*, the song *All You Need is Love* was played on several jukeboxes in some underground passages beneath the village.

2 They Sang *Yesterday*

The most recorded song in history is *Yesterday*, with approximately 1,200 versions worldwide by a whole host of artists who interpret the number in a variety of ways. Below is a list of fifty popular artists who have recorded the number:

1   Elvis Presley
2   Frank Sinatra
3   Diana Ross & The Supremes
4   Smokey Robinson & The Miracles
5   Tom Jones
6   Gladys Knight & The Pips
7   The Temptations
8   Mary Wells
9   Andy Williams
10 Liberace
11 Count Basie
12 Ella Fitzgerald
13 Sarah Vaughan
14 Oscar Peterson
15 Anita O'Day
16 Errol Garner
17 James Brown
18 Dionne Warwick
19 Marvin Gaye
20 Otis Redding
21 Jack Jones
22 Johnny Mathis
23 Al Martino
24 Perry Como
25 Nat King Cole
26 Pat Boone
27 Connie Francis
28 Brenda Lee
29 Chet Atkins
30 Floyd Kramer
31 Jan & Dean

32 Dr. John
33 Tennessee Ernie Ford
34 Tammy Wynette
35 Burl Ives
36 Marty Robbins
37 Percy Faith
38 James Last
39 Chris Montez
40 The Sandpipers
41 The Smothers Brothers
42 Jose Feliciano
43 P. P. Arnold
44 Cilla Black
45 Val Doonican
46 David Essex
47 Marianne Faithfull
48 Matt Monro
49 The Seekers
50 David & Jonathan

3 Inspiration

John and Paul drew their inspiration from many sources – people, places, incidents. Some were only the catalyst which led to a song, others were the entire theme of the number. Here are some of the sources of inspiration behind these songs:

Sexy Sadie The Maharishi Mahesh Yogi. John originally wanted to call the song *Maharishi* but was advised against it.

Dear Prudence John's observations about Prudence Farrow, sister of film star Mia Farrow, whom he thought took her meditation too seriously at the Rishikesh Ashram.

And I Love Her Jane Asher – an inspiration to Paul for several years.

I'm Looking Through You Jane Asher – by then no longer thought of in a loving vein – this was penned after the romance had died.

Eleanor Rigby First inspired by the name Daisy Hawkins which Paul spotted above a Bristol shopfront.

Dr. Robert An observation of a doctor in New York who prescribed pills too readily.

She Said, She Said Actor Peter Fonda made a strange remark to John whilst at a Hollywood party. John, who was on his second LSD trip, used the phrase to weave this song.

Being For The Benefit Of Mr. Kite The entire title came from the text on an unusual poster which John bought in an antique shop in Kent.

Blue Jay Way Name of a street in Los Angeles. George Harrison penned the number, using the street name, while he was waiting for Derek Taylor to turn up for an appointment.

Her Majesty Paul's tribute to Queen Elizabeth II, albeit a short one at only 23 seconds in length!

Norwegian Wood About an affair John had while he was still married to Cynthia and written in an ambiguous way in order to keep the affair secret.

Nowhere Man Actually arose because of a lack of inspiration. John's mind literally went blank. He became depressed and thought of himself as a 'nowhere man'.

Penny Lane Paul's tribute to an actual Liverpool Street, close by where both he and John grew up.

Strawberry Fields Forever A Victorian house and grounds near to where John grew up, a place where he attended garden parties.

Lucy In The Sky With Diamonds A painting by John's son Julian. John asked him who the subject was and Julian replied, 'It's Lucy in the sky with diamonds'.

Getting Better Jimmy Nicol, who temporarily replaced a sick Ringo Starr during the Beatles' world tour, used this phrase often. Paul remembered it when it came to writing a song.

She's Leaving Home The entire theme came from a story in the *Daily Mail* newspaper.

When I'm Sixty Four A tribute to Paul's father Jim McCartney, penned by Paul for his Dad's 64th birthday.

Lovely Rita Inspired by the remark of an American visitor to London who called the female traffic wardens 'meter maids'.

Good Morning Good Morning The tune arose when John heard a cornflake commerical on the radio.

A Day in the Life Two sources of inspiration, both from

stories in the *Daily Mail* newspaper. The first concerned 4,000 holes found in Blackburn, a town in Lancashire. The second was the report of the death in a car accident of Guinness heir Tara Browne, who had been a friend of the individual members of the Beatles.

Martha My Dear Paul's late-lamented English sheepdog found immortality in song.

Hey Jude Inspired by the name Julian. Paul was on his way to see Julian Lennon and began to hum the phrase 'Hey Jules', which eventually became 'Hey Jude'.

Happiness is A Warm Gun John saw this entire phrase on the cover of a gun magazine.

Do You Want To Know A Secret An early song of John's, inspired by his memories of a Disney film, although, years later, he couldn't remember whether it was *Cinderella* or *Fantasia*.

From Me To You Iris Caldwell, sister of Beatles friend Rory Storm and a former girl friend of Paul McCartney, claimed that Paul had written the song for her.

Michelle Inspired by Michelle Howard, daughter of Anthony Howard, who worked for the Beatles.

4 Their BBC Radio Recordings

The Beatles made their BBC radio recording debut on 7th March 1962 and during the next 3 years performed no less than eighty-eight different numbers on more than fifty radio appearances. A compilation to celebrate those years was first broadcast on BBC's Radio One on 7th March 1982, some 20 years after their first broadcast. It was retransmitted in greater length and in FM quality Entitled *The Beatles At The Beeb*, the show was produced by Jeff Griffin, assisted by Kevin Howlett. Kevin also wrote the book *The Beatles At The Beeb*, published in 1982 by BBC Publications. The eighty-eight numbers the group performed were:

1 *All My Loving*
2 *And I Love Her*
3 *Anna (Go To Him)*

George: 'Did you know that the Beatles first recorded for BBC Radio on March 7th 1962?' John: 'I don't wish to know that!'

 4 *Ask Me Why*
 5 *Baby It's You*
 6 *Beautiful Dreamer*
 7 *Besame Mucho*
 8 *Boys*
 9 *Can't Buy Me Love*
10 *Carol*
11 *Chains*
12 *Clarabella*
13 *Crying, Waiting, Hoping*
14 *Devil In Her Heart*
15 *Dizzy Miss Lizzie*
16 *Don't Ever Change*
17 *Do You Want To Know A Secret*
18 *Dream Baby*
19 *Everybody's Trying To Be My Baby*
20 *From Me To You*
21 *Glad All Over*
22 *A Hard Day's Night*
23 *The Hippy Hippy Shake*

24 *Honey Don't*
25 *The Honeymoon Song*
26 *I Call Your Name*
27 *I Feel Fine*
28 *If I Fell*
29 *I Forgot To Remember To Forget*
30 *I Got A Woman*
31 *I Got To Find My Baby*
32 *I Just Don't Understand*
33 *I'll Be On My Way*
34 *I'll Follow the Sun*
35 *I'll Get You*
36 *I'm A Loser*
37 *I'm Gonna Sit Right Down And Cry (Over You)*
38 *I'm Happy Just To Dance With You*
39 *I'm Talking About You*
40 *I Saw Her Standing There*
41 *I Should Have Known Better*
42 *I Wanna Be Your Man*
43 *I Want To Hold Your Hand*
44 *Johnny B. Goode*
45 *Kansas City*
46 *Keep Your Hands Off My Baby*
47 *Lend Me Your Comb*
48 *Lonesome Tears In My Eyes*
49 *Long Tall Sally*
50 *Love Me Do*
51 *Lucille*
52 *Matchbox*
53 *Memphis Tennessee*
54 *Misery*
55 *Money*
56 *The Night Before*
57 *Nothin' Shakin (But The Leaves On The Trees)*
58 *Ooh! My Soul*
59 *A Picture Of You*
60 *Please Mr. Postman*
61 *Please Please Me*
62 *P.S. I Love You*

63 *Rock & Roll Music*
64 *Roll Over Beethoven*
65 *She Loves You*
66 *She's A Woman*
67 *A Shot of Rhythm & Blues*
68 *Slow Down*
69 *So How Come (No One Loves Me)*
70 *Soldier Of Love*
71 *Some Other Guy*
72 *Sure To Fall (In Love With You)*
73 *Sweet Little Sixteen*
74 *A Taste Of Honey*
75 *Thank You Girl*
76 *That's All Right Mama*
77 *There's A Place*
78 *Things We Said Today*
79 *This Boy*
80 *Ticket To Ride*
81 *Till There Was You*
82 *To Know Her Is To Love Her*
83 *Too Much Monkey Business*
84 *Twist & Shout*
85 *Words Of Love*
86 *You Can't Do That*
87 *Young Blood*
88 *You Really Got A Hold On Me*

5 Extended Players

There were thirteen Beatles EPs issued in Britain during the sixties:

1 **Twist & Shout**
Tracks: *Twist & Shout; A Taste Of Honey; Do You Want To Know A Secret; There's A Place.* It was issued on Parlophone 8882 on 12th July 1963 and reached No. 2 in the charts.

2 **The Beatles Hits**
Tracks: *From Me To You; Thank You Girl; Please Please Me;*

Love Me Do. It was issued on Parlophone GEP 8880 on 6th September 1963 and reached No. 14 in the charts.

   3   *The Beatles (No. 1)*
Tracks: *I Saw Her Standing There; Misery; Anna (Go To Him); Chains*. It was issued on Parlophone GEP 8883 on 1st November 1963 and reached No. 12 in the charts.

   4   *All My Loving*
Tracks: *All My Loving; Ask Me Why; Money (That's What I Want); P.S. I Love You*. It was issued on Parlophone GEP 8891 on 7th February 1964 and also reached No. 12 in the charts.

   5   *Long Tall Sally*
Tracks: *Long Tall Sally; I Call Your Name; Slow Down; Matchbox*. It was issued on Parlophone GEP 8913 on 19th June 1964 and reached No. 14 in the charts.

   6   *A Hard Day's Night*
Tracks: *I Should Have Known Better; If I Fell; Tell Me Why; And I Love Her*. It was issued on Parlophone GEP 8920 on 4th November 1964 and reached No. 34 in the charts.

   6   *A Hard Day's Night No. 2*
Tracks: *Anytime At All; I'll Cry Instead; Things We Said Today; When I Get Home*. It was issued on Parlophone GEP 8924 on 6th November 1964.

   8   *Beatles For Sale*
Tracks: *No Reply; I'm A Loser; Rock & Roll Music; Eight Days A Week*. It was issued on Parlophone GEP 8931 on 6th April 1965.

   9   *Beatles For Sale No 2*
Tracks: *I'll Follow The Sun; Baby's In Black; Words Of Love; I Don't Want To Spoil The Party*. It was issued on Parlophone GEP 8938 on 4th June 1965.

   10   *Beatles Million Sellers*
Tracks: *She Loves You; I Want To Hold Your Hand; Can't Buy Me Love; I Feel Fine*. It was issued on Parlophone GEP 8946 on 6th December 1965.

   11   *Yesterday*
Tracks: *Act Naturally; You Like Me Too Much; Yesterday; Its Only Love*. It was issued on Parlophone GEP 8 on 4th March 1966.

12 Nowhere Man

Tracks: *Nowhere Man; Drive My Car; Michelle; You Won't See Me*. It was issued on Parlophone GEP 8952 on 8th July 1966.

13 *Magical Mystery Tour*

Tracks: *Magical Mystery Tour; Your Mother Should Know; I Am The Walrus; The Fool On The Hill; Flying; Blue Jay Way*. It was issued on Parlophone SMMT 1/2 as a set of two EPs on 8th December 1967 and reached No. 2 in the charts.

6 Chart Treat Down Under

The impact of the Beatles in 1964 was not confined to Europe and the USA. When the Australian charts were published on 27th March 1964, the first six positions were:

No. 1   *I Saw Her Standing There* The Beatles
No. 2   *Love Me Do* The Beatles
No. 3   *Roll Over Beethoven* The Beatles
No. 4   *All My Loving* The Beatles
No. 5   *She Loves You* The Beatles
No. 6   *I Want To Hold Your Hand* The Beatles

7 Ringo's Films

The critical kudos in the reviews of *A Hard Days Night* went to Ringo Starr, who critics believed was a natural actor with a tragi-comic style. He went on to appear in more films than any other member of the Beatles.

A Hard Day's Night (1964) The first, and still the most popular, Beatles' film. Ringo garnered the best reviews and was given his own scenes where he wanders around an area of London meeting people by a canal and in a pub to the backing of *Ringo's Theme*.

Help! (1965) Ringo is the central figure of the Beatles' first colour movie. He is pursued by a fanatical religious sect who intended to sacrifice him because he is wearing a sacred ring.

For a man who liked *Alley Oop*, he sure digs the *Caveman* style!

Candy (1968) Ringo's first solo venture in filmdom in a story based on Terry Southern's updating of the *Candide* classic. Blonde-haired Ewa Aulin plays the title role, an innocent seduced by a range of randy men, including Richard Burton as a University professor and Marlon Brando as a yogi. Ringo's cameo role was that of Emmanuel, a Mexican gardener.

Let It Be (1970) The documentary that showed the tensions that had begun to exist within the group. Ringo took a back seat in this film which is a sad record of the Beatles' final times together.

The Magic Christian (1970) Another film based on a Terry Southern novel, with Ringo portraying the adopted son of the world's richest man. Peter Sellers played his Dad and in one scene Ringo is escorted by a whip-wielding Raquel Welch through a galley of oar-pulling topless girls.

200 Motels (1971) Tony Palmer directed this film, which starred Frank Zappa. Ringo also portrayed Frank Zappa in the movie in addition to appearing as a dwarf.

Born To Boogie (1972) Ringo's directorial debut in this Apple film which starred Marc Bolan. Ringo also included himself, Elton John and Keith Moon in the movie.

That'll Be The Day (1973) Evocative British rock film with a bittersweet script by Ray Connolly and Ringo's most memorable performance to date. A pity he refused to continue his portrayal of Mike in the sequel *Stardust*.

Son Of Dracula (1974) Ringo turned producer for this horror spoof in which he co-starred with Harry Nilsson. He portrayed Merlin The Magician and Harry portrayed the vampire, Count Downe. Another Apple film.

Harry & Ringo's Night Out (1974) Ringo once again teams up with Harry Nilsson in a film which received little or no distribution.

Lisztomania (1975) Another of Ken Russell's 'over-the-top' movies with Roger Daltrey portraying Franz Liszt and Paul Nicholas as Richard Wagner, Ringo portrayed the Pope with no attempt at disguising his Liverpool accent.

Sextette (1976) Odd feature film starring Mae West which was never properly distributed, although it ended up regularly on the Art House circuit and is now available on video. Ringo co-starred, Tony Curtis guested and there were cameo appearances from Alice Cooper and Keith Moon.

The Last Waltz (1978) Martin Scorsese's record of the Band's farewell performance at the Winterland, San Francisco, with Ringo appearing with Bob Dylan and Ron Wood to augment the Band on the number *I Shall Be Released*.

Blindman (1972) Spanish Western in which Ringo stars as Candy, son of a bandit chief who has kidnapped fifty young women who were under the protection of a blind gunslinger.

The Kids Are Alright (1979) A documentary film covering 15 years in the career of the Who. Ringo is one of the group's guests in the film.

Caveman (1980) Starring role for Ringo as Atouk in this spoof, set one zillion years ago. The skinny caveman Atouk leads a band of misfits to triumph over the brawny, macho cave bullies. His future wife Barbara Bach co-starred, but lost her man.

The Cooler (1981) 13-minute short directed by Lol Creme and Kevin Godley featuring three numbers from *Stop and Smell The Roses* and appearances from Ringo and Barbara and Paul and Linda McCartney.

Princess Daisy (1983) Ringo and Barbara portray an unusual married couple in this lush television dramatisation of the best-selling novel about love and lust in the world's capital cities.

Give My Regards To Broad Street (1984) Paul McCartney's first major feature film, with guest roles for Ringo and Barbara.

8 *American Top Ten* Rock Idols

The American TV show *American Top Ten* ran one of their occasional 'special edition' polls in 1982 – *The Top Ten Male Performers Of The Rock Era*. The results were:

No. 1 Elvis Presley
No. 2 Paul McCartney
No. 3 John Lennon
No. 4 Stevie Wonder
No. 5 Mick Jagger
No. 6 Michael Jackson
No. 7 Pat Boone
No. 8 Frankie Valli
No. 9 Elton John
No. 10 Ricky Nelson

9 In The *NME* Polls

The *New Musical Express* was Britain's leading music weekly during the sixties and seventies and the Beatles featured prominently in their annual readers' polls. At one time, the publication ran 'Poll Winners' Concerts' at Wembley, on which the Beatles appeared on a few occasions. Among the poll results which featured the Fab Four were:

Single Of The Year
    1963 *She Loves You*
    1966 *Eleanor Rigby*
    1968 *Hey Jude*
    1970 *My Sweet Lord* George Harrison

Album Of The Year
    1970 *Let It Be*

Bass Guitarist Of The Year
    1972 Paul McCartney
    1973 Paul McCartney
    1974 Paul McCartney
    1976 Paul McCartney

Vocal Personality Of The Year
    1965 John Lennon

World Vocal Group
    1963 The Beatles
    1964 The Beatles
    1965 The Beatles
    1967 The Beatles
    1968 The Beatles
    1969 The Beatles

UK Vocal Group
    1963 The Beatles
    1964 The Beatles
    1965 The Beatles
    1966 The Beatles
    1967 The Beatles
    1968 The Beatles
    1969 The Beatles
    1970 The Beatles

10 Imitators

Despite having established copyright on a distinctive name, the Beatles were to generate many imitators, some of whom were to use the title quite blatantly. There was even a group who called themselves The Beatles and issued a disc, *The Girl I Love*, in 1965 – and another artist called himself John Lennon and issued a single called *Ram You Hard* in 1970. There was also a John Lemon and a duo who called themselves John & Paul. The following are all genuine acts or recording artists:

   The American Beatles
   The Canadian Beatles
   The Japanese Beatles
   The German Beatles
   The Sex Beatles
   The Bootleg Beatles
   The Female Beatles
   The Beetles
   Beatles Costello

The Rutles produced what was probably the finest tribute to the Beatles.

The Beatles Revival Band
The Beatles Buddies
The Beatle Bugs
The Beatle-Ettes
Little Lady Beatles
Judy Stewart & Her Beatle Buddies
The U.S. Beatlewigs

11 *Desert Island Discs*

Paul McCartney's choices during his appearance on BBC Radio's long-running *Desert Island Discs*, hosted by Roy Plomley. The asterisk identifies the record the castaway would have if he were only allowed a single disc on the island.

Heartbreak Hotel   Elvis Presley
Sweet Little Sixteen   Chuck Berry
Courtly Dances From Gloriana   Julian Bream Consort
Be-Bop-A-Lula   Gene Vincent
Searchin'   The Coasters
Tutti Frutti   Little Richard
Walking In The Park With Eloise   The Country Hams
Beautiful Boy   John Lennon

The luxury: A guitar. The book: *Linda's Pictures*.

12 *Love Me Do* At No. 1

Love Me Do was the Beatles very first chart entry, although it was not a massive hit in its first year of release. It reached its highest position of No. 17 in one London music paper for 1 week only, was No. 27 for 1 week in another, but managed to at least make its presence felt in all four London musical weeklies, reaching No. 24 in *Disc* and No. 32 in *Record Mirror*, in addition to the *Melody Maker* and *New Musical Express* placings. However, as was to be expected, it reached No. 1 soon after release in the North's only music paper: *Mersey Beat*. The Full

Top 20 of the 18th October 1962 issue was as follows:

No. 1 *Love Me Do*   The Beatles
No. 2 *Telstar*   The Tornadoes
No. 3 *The Locomotion*   Little Eva
No. 4 *It Might As Well Rain Until September*   Carole King
No. 5 *Sheila*   Tommy Roe
No. 6 *Ramblin' Rose*   Nat King Cole
No. 7 *She's Not You*   Elvis Presley
No. 8 *Devil Woman*   Marty Robbins
No. 9 *What Now My Love*   Shirley Bassey
No. 10 *You Don't Know Me*   Ray Charles
No. 11 *I Remember You*   Frank Ifield
No. 12 *It'll Be Me*   Cliff Richard
No. 13 *Let's Dance*   Chris Montez
No. 14 *Reminiscing*   Buddy Holly
No. 15 *Don't That Beat All*   Adam Faith
No. 16 *Things*   Bobby Darin
No. 17 *Venus In Blue Jeans*   Mark Wynter
No. 18 *Speedy Gonzales*   Pat Boone
No. 19 *Send Me The Pillow*   Johnny Tillotson
No. 20 *It's Started All Over Again*   Brenda Lee

13 Drums Along The Mersey

There are a handful of drummers who can claim that they once played, however fleetingly, with the Beatles. They include:

Norman Chapman Sat in with the group in the days when they had no permanent drummer, but National Service cut short his chance of remaining with them.

Johnny Hutchinson Performed with them on one or two occasions, most notably at the Larry Parne's auditions in the Wyvern club when Stu Sutcliffe played bass guitar. Johnny later became the mainman behind the Big Three.

Tommy Moore Toured Scotland with them for a few weeks in

'By George, I think he's got it!'

1960 when they backed Johnny Gentle. His girfriend persuaded him that there was no future in staying. He died in 1981.

Pete Best Joined them in August 1960 and soon became one of the most popular members of the band. During the next 2 years, he travelled to Hamburg with them and was part of their growth when they developed into the most popular group in Liverpool.

Andy White Session musician who was booked by George

Martin to play on their debut record. Their new drummer Ringo Starr wasn't too happy about this state of events, so he was allowed to play on one of the cuts: so two versions of *Love Me Do* have been released – one featuring Andy on drums, the other with Ringo.

Jimmy Nicol For a few weeks, he substituted for Ringo during the Beatles' 1964 world tour, appearing in the Netherlands, Hong Kong and Australia with them until Ringo, who had been suffering from tonsillitis, returned to his drum stool.

14 The *NME* Concerts

The leading British musical weekly *New Musical Express* presented a series of concerts in the sixties featuring artists who topped their annual popularity polls. The concerts, known as 'The Poll Winners' Concerts, were all held in Wembley and the Beatles appeared on the following dates:

Empire Pool, Wembley: 21st April 1963
Wembley Stadium: 26th April 1964
Wembley Stadium: 11th April 1965
Wembley Stadium: 1st May 1966

Their 1965 concert was screened on ABC TV and networked throughout the UK on 18th April of that year and their 1966 appearance was their last concert show in the UK.

15 Lennon's Literary Licence

John Lennon was an avid reader and his collection of books covered many subjects. A handful of books had a profound influence on him and some of them inspired his songs.

Just William By Richmael Crompton. Just one of a series of books about a schoolboy scamp which John devoured in his youth . . . and possibly influenced his own mischievous schoolboy pranks!

Alice's Adventures In Wonderland and *Through The Looking Glass* By Lewis Carroll. The wonderful surrealist images and the intriguing characters (i.e. *The Walrus And The Carpenter*) obviously influenced the material John compiled for his two books. Carroll's shadow is also apparent in *I Am The Walrus*.

The Doors of Perception By Aldous Huxley. This work presented the heightening of awareness by the use of hallucinogenic drugs in a fascinating way and possibly aided John's belief that he could enhance his creativity with the use of LSD.

Grapefruit By Yoko Ono. A slim volume of Yoko's conceptual ideas which John kept by his bedside. He often flicked through its pages, becoming frustrated or inspired by the unusual content of the short poems.

The First Sex By Elizabeth Gould Davis. A book which Yoko urged him to read which presented him with an insight into the role of woman as a second-class citizen and possibly influenced numbers such as *Woman Is The Nigger Of The World*.

Mind Games by Robert Masters and Jean Houston. Techniques of enhancing creativity without the use of drugs and an obvious influence on his *Mind Games* album.

Primal Therapy: The Cure for Neurosis by Arthur Janov, A revolutionary method of psychiatry, tracing current psychological problems to childhood memories and releasing them with a 'primal scream'. After undergoing personal therapy with Janov, John wrote many songs which were included on his *John Lennon/Plastic Ono Band* album, which has been called his 'Primal Album'.

16 American Misses

Not every Beatles' release was a hit in the USA. In fact, a number of Beatles and Beatles-related singles and albums failed to enter any of the three major US charts at all. Here is a list of their American flops:

SINGLES
My Bonnie c/w *The Saints* Tony Sheridan & The Beat Brothers

Please Please Me c/w *Ask Me Why*   The Beatles (initial release)
Sweet Georgia Brown c/w *Take Out Some Insurance On Me Baby*   The Beatles featuring Tony Sheridan
Walking In The Park With Eloise c/w *Bridge Over The River Suite*   The Country Hams
This Guitar c/w *Maya Love*   George Harrison
Drowning In The Sea Of Love c/w *Just A Dream*   Ringo Starr
Heart On My Sleeve c/w *Who Needs Love*   Ringo Starr
Wonderful Christmastime c/w *Rudolph The Red-Nosed Reggae*   Paul McCartney
Private Property c/w *Stop And Take The Time To Smell The Roses*   Ringo Starr

ALBUMS
Ain't She Sweet   The Beatles
Ed Rudy With The New U.S. Tour
The Beatles Tapes   (David Wigg Interviews)
Beatle Talk   (Red Robinson Interviews)

17 Mersey Moments

The Beatles weren't the first Merseyside artists to reach the charts. The area had always been acknowledged as a breeding ground for entertainers, and singers from the Liverpool area have been making appearances in the British charts almost since the inception of record charts in the UK by the *New Musical Express* in 1952.

This listing mainly concerns Liverpool acts who have made chart appearances between the years 1960 and 1970. Most, though not all, had been members of the Mersey Beat scene.

Liverpool singer **Lita Rosa** made her chart debut with (*How Much Is*) *That Doggie In The Window*, which topped the charts in March 1953. Her other fifties' hits included *Hey There* and *Jimmy Unknown*. The fifties was the era of crooners in the UK, with most of the major singers having experienced a period as

The Mersey Sound lives on! The Swinging Blue Jeans are as 'in demand' as ever.

vocalist with a dance band. The Liverpudlian who made the most impact was **Frankie Vaughan** who, between 1954 and 1968 had a total of thirty-one chart entries, including his 1961 No. 1 hit *Tower of Strength*. He also starred in a film, set in Liverpool: *These Dangerous Years*. The other major Liverpool singer of the period was **Michael Holliday**, a crooner in the Crosby/Como vein who died at the beginning of the sixties. He had twelve chart entries between 1956 and 1960 including two chart-toppers: *The Story Of My Life* and *Starry Eyed*.

Liverpool is also famous for comedians, a few of them also finding chart success. The most notable was **Ken Dodd**, whose hilarious encounter with the Beatles was screened in January 1983 in Granada TV's *The Early Beatles*. He once presented me with a certificate, making me an honourable Diddyman for my services to Liverpool via *Mersey Beat*. Ken had a string of hits lasting until the late seventies. In the sixties alone he had fourteen chart hits, including his No. 1 chart-topper *Tears*. **Norman Vaughan** is another comedian who entered the charts with a minor hit, *Swingin' In The Rain* in 1962.

Another mainstream pop act from Liverpool were **The Vernons Girls**, originally formed from workers at Vernons

33

Football Pools. There were numerous line-up changes and they had five chart hits between 1962 and 1963, their most famous being *Lover Please*.

A Liverpool singer who became a major British rock and roll idol was the late **Billy Fury**. Billy did not experience performing on the Mersey Beat scene as he became famous literally overnight as a protégé of Larry Parnes who controlled a stable of rock and roll stars. Billy had twenty-six chart hits between 1959 and 1966, his highest position being No. 2 with *Jealousy*.

There were scores of Mersey Beat artists who entered the recording studios in the wake of **The Beatles**, but only a relative handful of them achieved chart success.

The Mersey Beat acts who charted in the sixties were:

The Big Three Their debut single *Some Other Guy* (Decca F11614) reached No 37 in April 1963 and in July of the same year they reached No. 22 with *By The Way* (Decca F11689).

Cilla Black She was the only female singer from Liverpool to make a major impact in the sixties. Her hits were *Love Of The Loved* (Parlophone R5065) which reached No. 35 in October 1963. She reached No. 1 in February 1964 with *Anyone Who Had A Heart* (Parlophone R5101) and also topped the charts with *You're My World* (Parlophone R5133) in May of the same year. *It's For You* (Parlophone R5162) reached No. 7 in August 1964. *You've Lost That Lovin' Feeling* (Parlophone R5225) reached No. 2 in January, 1965. *I've Been Wrong Before* (Parlophone R5265) reached No. 17 in April 1965, *Love's Just A Broken Heart* (Parlophone R5395) reached No. 5 in January 1966. *Alfie* (Parlophone R5427) reached No. 9 in March 1966. *Don't Answer Me* (Parlophone 5463) reached No. 6 in June 1966. *A Fool Am I* (Parlophone R5515) reached No. 13 in October 1966. *What Good Am I* (ParlophoneR5608) reached No. 24 in June 1967. *I Only Live To Love You* (Parlophone R5652) reached No. 26 in November 1967. *Step Inside Love* (Parlophone R5674) reached No. 8 in March 1968. *Where is Tomorrow* (Parlophone R5706) reached No. 40 in June 1968. *Surround Yourself With Sorrow* (Parlophone R5759) reached No. 3 in February 1969. *Conversations* (Parlophone R5785) reached No. 7 in July 1969 and *If I Thought You'd Change Your Mind* (Parlophone R5820) reached No. 20

The Fourmost disbanded after more than twenty years together; they were one of Liverpool's most hilarious bands.

in December 1969. Cilla had a few further hits in the early seventies.

The Cryin' Shames A group at the tail end of the Mersey scene, they had a solitary hit, *Please Stay* (Decca F12340), which reached No. 26 in March 1966.

The Dennisons They had two hits: *Be My Girl* (Decca F11691) reached No. 46 in April 1963 and *Walkin' The Dog* (Decca F11880), which reached No. 36 in May 1964.

The Escorts had one hit *The One to Cry* (Fontana TF 474) which reached No. 49 in July 1964.

The Fourmost made their chart debut with the Lennon & McCartney song *Hello Little Girl* (Parlophone R5056) which reached No. 9 in September 1963. *I'm In Love* (Parlophone R5078) reached No. 17 in December 1963. *A Little Lovin'* (Parlophone R5128) reached No. 6 in April 1964. *Now I Can Tell Them* (Parlophone R5157) reached No. 33 in August 1964. *Baby I Need Your Lovin'* (Parlophone R5194) reached No. 24 in November 1964) and their final hit was *Girls Girls Girls* (Parlophone R5379), which reached No. 33 in December 1965.

David Garrick was a solo artist who was originally manager of a Mersey band, The Dions. His hits were *Lady Jane* (Piccadilly 7N 35317) which reached No. 28 in June 1966 and *Dear Mrs. Applebee* (Piccadilly 7N 35335), which reached No. 22 in September of the same year.

Gerry & The Pacemakers were the Beatles' close friends and rivals and achieved the record of three consecutive No. 1s with their first three releases – a record which has still not been beaten. Their hits were *How Do You Do It?* (Columbia DB 4987), which reached No. 1 in March 1963. *I Like It* (Columbia DB 7041) which reached No. 1 in May 1963 and *You'll Never Walk Alone* (Columbia DB 7126) which reached No. 1 in October of the same year. *I'm The One* (Columbia DB 7189) reached No. 2 in January 1964. *Don't Let The Sun Catch You Crying* (Columbia DB 7268) reached No. 6 in April 1964. *It's Gonna Be Alright* (Columbia DB 7353) reached No. 24 in September 1964, *Ferry 'Cross The Mersey* (Columbia DB 7437) reached No. 8 in December 1964. *I'll Be There* (Columbia DB 7504) reached No. 12 in March 1965 and *Walk Hand In Hand* (Columbia DB 7738) reached No. 29 in November 1965.

Billy J. Kramer was another Brian Epstein artist who debuted with a Lennon and McCartney composition. *Do You Want To Know A Secret?* (Parlophone R5023) reached No. 2 in May 1963. *Bad To Me* (Parlophone R5049) reached No. 1 in August 1963. *I'll Keep You Satisfied* (Parlophone R5073) reached No. 4 in November 1963. *Little Children* (Parlophone R5105) reached No. 1 in February 1964. *From A Window* (Parlophone R5156) reached No. 10 in July 1964 and *Trains And Boats and Planes* (Parlophone R5285) reached No. 12 in May 1965.

The Long And the Short had two minor hits. *The Letter* (Decca F11959) which reached No. 30 in September 1964 and *Choc Ice* (Decca F12043), which reached No. 40 in December of the same year.

The Merseybeats, named after the newspaper which I launched, made their chart debut with *It's Love That Really Counts* (Fontana TF 412) which reached No. 24 in September 1963. *I Think Of You* (Fontana TF 431) reached No. 5 in January 1964. *Don't Turn Around* (Fontana TF 459) reached No. 13 in April 1964. *Wishin' and Hopin'* (Fontana TF 482) reached No. 13 in July 1964. *Last Night* (Fontana TF 504) reached No. 40 in November 1964. *I Love You Yes I Do* (Fontana TF 607) reached No. 25 in October 1965 and *I Stand Accused* (Fontana TF 645) reached No. 38 in January 1966. The group disbanded and the two lead singers, Tony Crane and Billy Kinsley, recorded as a duo, changing their name to **The Merseys** and had a solitary hit with *Sorrow* (Fontana TF 694), which reached No. 4 in April 1966. Billy Kinsley was to enjoy several further chart entries in the seventies with a new band, **Liverpool Express**.

The Mojos had several line-up changes and actor Lu Collins was once a member. Their first hit *Everything's All Right* (Decca F11853) reached No. 9 in March 1964. *Why Not Tonight* (Decca F11918) reached No. 25 in June 1964 and finally *Seven Daffodils* (Decca F11959) reached No. 30 in September 1964.

Tommy Quickly another Epstein solo artist, had a single hit *Wild Side Of Life* (Pye 7N 15708) which reached No. 33 in October 1964.

The Scaffold were a comedy trio with Paul McCartney's brother Mike McGear in the line-up. They had their first hit with *Thank U Very Much* (Parlophone R5643) which reached No. 4 in November 1967. *Do You Remember* (Parlophone R5679) reached No. 34 in March 1968. *Lily The Pink* (Parlophone R5734) reached No. 1 in November 1968. *Gin Gan Goolie* (Parlophone R5812) was their last hit of the sixties and reached No. 50 in December 1969. Their 1974 chart hit was *Liverpool Lou*.

The Searchers were a very popular quartet who are still performing. They reached No. 1 with their debut record *Sweets For My Sweet* (Pye 7N 15533) in June 1963. *Sugar and Spice* (Pye 7N 15566) reached No. 2 in October 1963 and *Sweet Nothins*, one of their German recordings, was issued on Philips BF 1274 and reached No. 48, also in October 1963. *Needles and Pins* (Pye 7N 15594) reached the No. 1 position in January 1964. *Don't Throw Your Love Away* (Pye 7N 15630) also reached No. 1 In April 1964. *Someday We're Gonna Love Again* (Pye 7N 15670) reached No. 11 in July 1964. *When You Walk In The Room* (Pye 7N 15694) reached No. 3 in September 1964. *What Have They Done To The Rain* (Pye 7N 15739) reached

No. 13 in December 1964. *Goodbye My Love* (Pye 7N 15794) reached No. 4 in March 1965. *He's Got No Love* (Pye 7N 15878) reached No. 12 in July 1965. *When I Get Home* (Pye 7N 15950) reached No. 35 in October 1965. *Take Me For What I'm Worth* (Pye 7N 15992) reached No. 20 in December 1965. *Take It Or Leave It* (Pye 7N 17094) reached No. 31 in April 1966 and *Have You Ever Loved Somebody* (Pye 7N 17170) reached No. 48 in October 1966.

Denny Seyton & The Sabres had a solitary hit *The Way You Look Tonight* (Mercury MF 824), which reached No. 48 in September 1964.

The Swinging Blue Jeans made their chart debut with *It's Too Late Now* (HMV Pop 1170) which reached No. 30 in June 1963. *Hippy Hippy Shake* (HMV Pop 1242) reached No. 2 in December 1963. *Good Golly Miss Molly* (HMV Pop 1273) reached No. 11 in March 1964. *You're No Good* (HMV Pop 1304) reached No. 3 in June 1964 and *Don't Make Me Over* (HMV Pop 1501) reached No. 31 in January 1966.

The Undertakers were a very popular group locally in Liverpool but only had one minor hit, *Just A Little Bit* (Pye 7N 15607) which reached No. 49 in April 1964.

Tony Jackson, former singer with The Searchers, left to form his own band **The Vibrations** and had a minor hit *Bye Bye Baby* (Pye 7N 15685) which reached No. 38 in October 1964.

Trevor Morais drummer with Faron's Flamingos, left to join a trio called **The Peddlers**, who had minor hits with *Let The Sunshine In* (Philips BF 1375), which reached No. 50 in January 1965 and *Birth* (GBS 4449), which reached No. 17 in August 1969. They had one further hit *Girlie* in 1970.

The final sixties hitmaker from Liverpool used the pseudonym **Whistling Jack Smith** for his single *I Was Kaiser Bill's Batman*, which reached No. 5 in March 1967.

18 Books By Beatles

All four members of the Beatles had books published, although none were autobiographical. George attempted to portray his story through his recollection of his songs and the biographical section in *I, Me, Mine* was written by Derek Taylor from interviews conducted with George.

John Lennon *In His Own Write* was first published in the UK by Jonathan Cape in 1964 and in the USA by Simon & Schuster the same year. The French edition was called *En Flagrante Delire*. His second book *A Spaniard In The Works* was issued the following year by the same publishers. *In His Own Write* was adapted as a play and a book *In His Own Write: The Lennon Play* was issued, credited to John Lennon, Adrienne Kennedy and Victor Spinetti. Several paperback versions of both books contained in one volume have been published, including *The Penguin John Lennon*.

Paul McCartney The book *Paul McCartney Composer/Artist* was published in 1981 by Pavilion Books and is the nearest Paul has come to a book of his own. It contains his own illustrations to a large number of his songs, together with a personal introduction.

George Harrison *I, Me, Mine* was originally issued in a deluxe edition, limited to 2,000 copies, each of them personally signed. The book, by Genesis Publications, sold for £184, but is already believed to have become a collector's item and worth more than the original price. A cheaper, hardbound edition was published the following year in 1981 by W. H. Allen in the UK and Simon & Schuster in the USA.

Ringo Starr Ringo put his Pentax camera to good use when he began taking photographs of the Beatles in 1963. His book *Ringo's Photo Album* was first published in the USA in 1964. It is a rare book and contains seventy-five photographs taken by Ringo, together with an introductory letter.

19 Ringo For President

In 1964, when the Beatles made their initial, dynamic impact on the USA, there were shoals of novelty records issued. An indication of how popular Ringo Starr became during this period is found in the number of records about him, which far exceeded those dedicated to the other members. The American singles during the year 1964 alone included:

Ringo   The Weekend
Ringo   The Starlettes
Ringo   Bob Dean
Ringo Part One/Part Two   Carl & The Haircuts
My Ringo   The Rainbows
Ringo Ringo   Darlene Terri
Ringo, Dingo c/w *Here Comes Ringo*   The Tributes
R (Is For Ringo)   Tina Ferra
Ringo-Dear   Gary Ferrier
Ringo Beat   Ella Fitzgerald
Ringo Boy   Dori Peyton
Ringo's Jerk   Ron Ringo
Ringo's Walk   Joey & The Classics
Like Ringo   Dick Lord
Ringo's Dog   The Jack Dorsey Big Band
Go Go With Ringo   The Whippets
Ringo Did It   Veronica Lee & The Moniques
Where Did Ringo Go?   The Beatle Bugs
Ringo Comes To Town   Chug & Doug
I Want To Kiss Ringo Goodbye   Penny Valentine
Ringo, I Want To Know Your Secret   Pat Wynter
I Want Ringo For Christmas   The Four Sisters
Santa, Bring Me Ringo   Christine Hunter
A Tribute To Ringo Starr (The Other Ringo)   Larry Finnegan
You Can't Go Far Without A Guitar (Unless You're Ringo Starr)   Neil Sheppard
Ringo For President   Rolf Harris
Ringo For President   The Young World Singers
What's Wrong With Ringo?   The BonBugs (This girl group were later to re-emerge as The Shangri-Las with a huge hit *The Leader Of The Pack*.)
Bingo Ringo   Butler Daws (The man who provided the voice to the Huckleberry Hound character in the cartoons. In fact, copies of the single were actually credited to Huckleberry Hound.)
Ringo, I Love You   Bonnie Jo Mason (She changed her name to Cher – and this single was produced by Phil Spector.)
Minuet For Ringo   Viv Prince (This was released in the UK

only, a novelty disc by the drummer with The Pretty Things.)
Ringo, Ringo Little Starr was a track from the album *It's A Beatle World* by Al & Lou Marks Fisher and *Ringo's Theme* was a track by George Martin from the score of *A Hard Day's Night*.

Treat Him Tender Maureen was a single issued by Angie & The Chicklettes, when Ringo married Maureen Cox.

20 Vital Statistics

When any group or artist signs with a record company, the preparation of a biographical information sheet is an inevitable and essential way of providing basic information to the Press. When the Beatles first signed with Parlophone, an information sheet was compiled. Over the years, their tastes, ambitions and outlooks all changed, but their original Press handout remained to remind them of their personal opinions in 1962.

Paul McCartney
Date of birth   18th June 1942
Weight   11½st
Height   5ft 11in
Colour of eyes   Brown
Colour of hair   Dark brown
First professional appearance   In Liverpool
Recording company   EMI
Likes   Music, reading and writing songs
Hates   False and soft people, shaving
Favourite food   Steak and chips
Favourite clothes   Black polo-necked sweaters, suits, leather and suede
Favourite colour   Black
Favourite game   Motor racing
Favourite singers   Ray Charles, Peggy Lee
Favourite actor   Anthony Quinn
Favourite actress   Brigitte Bardot
Favourite companion   Current girlfriend
Ambition   To make money, and do well

If you've never eaten steak and chips at Joe's Cafe in Duke Street, you've never lived!

John Lennon
Date of birth   9th October 1940
Weight   11st
Height   5ft 11in
Colour of eyes   Brown
Colour of hair   Brown
First professional appearance   Club in Liverpool
Recording company   EMI
Likes   Music, books, painting, television
Hates   Thickheads and traditional jazz
Favourite food   Steak and chips, curries, and jelly
Favourite clothes   Dark-coloured in suede and leather
Favourite colour   Black
Favourite games   Ball games
Favourite singer   Carl Perkins, Chuck Berry, Kay Starr
Favourite actors   Marlon Brando, Peter Sellers
Favourite actress   Brigitte Bardot
Favourite companion   Blonde, intelligent girls
Ambition   'Money and everything'

George Harrison
Date of birth   25th February 1943
Weight   11st
Height   5ft 11in
Colour of eyes   Hazel
Colour of hair   Dark brown
First professional appearance   Night club in Liverpool
Recording company   EMI
Likes   Records, guitars, girls
Hates   A haircut, travelling on buses
Favourite food   Egg and chips
Favourite clothes   Casual
Favouite colour   Blue/black
Favourite game   Racing
Favourite singer   Eartha Kitt
Favourite actor   Marlon Brando
Favourite actress   Jean Simmons
Favourite companion   Girls
Ambition   To retire rich!

Ringo Starr
Date of birth   7th July 1940
Weight   10½st
Height   5ft 8in
Colour of eyes   Blue
Colour of hair   Brown
First professional appearance   Liverpool, 1962
Recording company   EMI
Likes   Fast cars, his parents and anyone who likes him!
Hates   Onions, motor bikes, Chinese food
Favourite food   Steak and chips
Favourite clothes   Sleek suits and ties
Favourite colour   Black
Favourite game   Racing
Favourite singer   Dinah Washington
Favourite actor   Paul Newman
Favourite actress   Brigitte Bardot
Favourite companion   Girls
Ambition   To get to the top

21 *American Top Ten*

A syndicated American television show. In a special 1981 edition of the programme, *American Top Ten* announced their list of the Top Ten British Recording Artists. They were :

No. 1 The Beatles
No. 2 The Rolling Stones
No. 3 The Bee Gees
No. 4 Elton John
No. 5 Paul McCartney
No. 6 Olivia Newton-John
No. 7 Herman's Hermits
No. 8 Andy Gibb
No. 9 The Dave Clark Five
No. 10 Rod Stewart

22 British Sixties Singles

Between 1962 and 1970 when the group ceased to exist, the Beatles had twenty-two singles issued in the UK:

1 *LOVE ME DO* c/w *P.S. I Love You* Issued on Parlophone R4949 on 5th October 1962. It reached No. 17 in the charts for 1 week only.

2 *PLEASE PLEASE ME* c/w *Ask Me Why* Issued on Parlophone R4983 on 12th January 1963. It reached No. 1 in the charts.

3 *FROM ME TO YOU* c/w *Thank You Girl* Issued on Parlophone R5015 on 11th April 1963. It reached No. 1 in the charts.

4 *SHE LOVES YOU* c/w *I'll Get You* Issued on Parlophone R5055 on 23rd August 1963. It reached No. 1 in the charts.

5 *I WANT TO HOLD YOUR HAND* c/w *This Boy* Issued on Parlophone R5084 on 29th November 1963. It reached No. 1 in the charts.

6 *CAN'T BUY ME LOVE* c/w *You Can't Do That* Issued

on Parlophone R5114 on 2nd March 1964. It reached No. 1 in the charts.

7 *A HARD DAY'S NIGHT* c/w *Things We Said Today* Issued on Parlophone R5160 on 10th July 1964. It reached No. 1 in the charts.

8 *I FEEL FINE* c/w *She's A Woman* Issued on Parlophone R5200 on 27th November 1964. It reached No. 1 in the charts.

9 *TICKET TO RIDE* c/w *Yes It Is* Issued on Parlophone R5265 on 9th April 1965. It reached No. 1 in the charts.

10 HELP! c/w *I'm Down* Issued on Parlophone R5305 on 23rd July 1965. It reached No. 1 in the charts.

11 *WE CAN WORK IT OUT/DAY TRIPPER* Double 'A' side. Issued on Parlophone R5389 on 3rd December 1965. It reached No. 1 in the charts.

12 *PAPERBACK WRITER* c/w *Rain* Issued on Parlophone R5452 on 10th June 1966. It reached No. 1 in the charts.

13 *ELEANOR RIGBY/YELLOW SUBMARINE* Double 'A' side. Issued on Parlophone R5493 on 8th August 1966. It reached No. 1 in the charts.

14 *PENNY LANE/STRAWBERRY FIELDS FOREVER* Double 'A' side. Issued of Parlophone R5570 on 17th February 1967. It reached No. 2 in the charts.

15 *ALL YOU NEED IS LOVE* c/w *Baby You're A Rich Man* Issued on Parlophone R5620 on 7th July 1967. It reached No. 1 in the charts.

16 *HELLO GOODBYE* c/w *I Am The Walrus* Issued on Parlophone R5655 on 14th November 1967. It reached No. 1 in the charts.

17 *LADY MADONNA* c/w *The Inner Light* Issued on Parlophone R5675 on 15th March 1968. It reached No. 1 in the charts.

18 *HEY JUDE* c/w *Revolution* Issued on Apple R5722 on 30th August 1968. It reached No. 2 in the charts.

19 *GET BACK* c/w *Don't Let Me Down* Issued on Apple R5777 on 15th April 1969. It reached No. 1 in the charts.

20 *THE BALLAD OF JOHN & YOKO* c/w *Old Brown Shoe* Issued on Apple R5786 on 30th May 1969. It reached No. 1 in the charts.

21 *SOMETHING* c/w *Come Together* Issued on Apple R5814 on 31st October 1969. It reached No. 4 in the charts.

22 *LET IT BE* c/w *You Know My Name (Look Up The Number)* Issued on Parlophone R6013 on 5th March 1970. It reached No. I in the charts.

23 *Band On The Run* Characters

Paul McCartney's December 1973 album featured nine characters caught in a spotlight on the cover of the sleeve. Apart from the three main members of Wings, Paul, Linda and Denny Laine, they comprised:

James Coburn Popular American movie star whose films range from, *The Magnificent Seven* to *Cross of Iron*. He lived with British singer/songwriter Lynsey De Paul for several years. Lynsey was also Ringo Starr's girl friend for a time.

John Conte Liverpool boxer who became Light Heavyweight Champion of the World. One of the many 'scousers' who kept Liverpudlian heads high in the wake of the Beatles.

Paul put the spotlight on some interesting characters on his *Band on the Run* album.

Christopher Lee Descendant of Charlemagne and the UK's premier horror movie character. Since his starring role in *Dracula* in 1958, he has portrayed most of the screen's immortal monsters, from Frankenstein's creation to Fu Manchu. He moved to the USA in the seventies where he has found success making TV movies.

Kenny Lynch British singer who had some minor hits in the sixties. A popular entertainer who was invited to No. 10 Downing Street by the Prime Minister, Harold Wilson. He recorded the Beatles' song *Misery*.

Clement Freud Descendant of the father of psychiatry, Sigmund Freud, he is also a Member of Parliament for the Liberal Party, an author and a television personality. His face is perhaps more familiar to viewers due to a certain TV commercial for dog food.

Michael Parkinson Former journalist from Yorkshire who found his greatest fame as a chat show host, with his *Parkinson* show running on BBC TV for over a decade. In 1983, he became a shareholder and one of the presenters of TV AM, a breakfast-time commerical TV station. When Mike accepted Paul's offer to appear on the record sleeve, he made Paul promise that he'd appear on his show one day.

24 Holding Hands

There have been scores of novelty versions of *I Want To Hold Your Hand*. Some artists decided to taken even greater licence with their spoof versions of the number, to the extent of altering the lyrics and title slightly, as on the following records:

Yes You Can Hold My Hand   The Teen Bugs
Just Hold My Hand   Paul Perryman
You Can Hold My Hand   Lafawn Paul
I Want To Bite Your Hand   Gene Moss
I Don't Want To Hold Your Hand   Homer & Jethro
I'll Let You Hold My Hand   The Bootles
Yes You Can Hold My Hand   The Beatle-Ettes
I Wanna Hold Your Hair   The Bagles

25 The Beatles in *Record World*

Record World was one of the three major music trade magazines in the USA during the sixties and seventies, the others being *Cashbox* and *Billboard*. Sadly, the publication folded in 1982. Here are the highest positions Beatles, solo-Beatles and Beatles-related records reached in the *Record World* charts.

SINGLES

She Loves You c/w *I'll Get by*	The Beatles	No. 1
Roll Over Beethoven c/w *Please Mr. Postman*	The Beatles	No. 35
I Want To Hold Your Hand c/w *I Saw Her Standing There*	The Beatles	No. 1
My Bonnie c/w *The Saints*	The Beatles	No. 31
Please Please Me c/w *From Me To You*	The Beatles	No. 3
All My Loving c/w *This Boy*	The Beatles	No. 32
Twist & Shout c/w *There's A Place*	The Beatles	No. 1
Can't Buy Me Love c/w *You Can't Do That*	The Beatles	No. 1
Do You Want To Know A Secret? c/w *Thank You Girl*	The Beatles	No. 3
Love Me Do c/w *P.S. I Love You*	The Beatles	No. 1
Ain't She Sweet c/w *Nobody's Child*	The Beatles	No. 13

A Hard Day's Night c/w *I Should Have Known Better*	The Beatles	No. 1
I'll Cry Instead c/w *I'm Happy Just To Dance* *With You*	The Beatles	No. 28
And I Love Her c/w *If I Fell*	The Beatles	No. 16
Matchbox c/w *Slow Down*	The Beatles	No. 22
I Feel Fine c/w *She's A Woman*	The Beatles	No. 1
Eight Days A Week c/w *I Don't Want To Spoil The Party*	The Beatles	No. 1
Ticket To Ride c/w *Yes It Is*	The Beatles	No. 1
Help! c/w *I'm Down*	The Beatles	No. 1
Yesterday c/w *Act Naturally*	The Beatles	No. 1
We Can Work It Out c/w *Day Tripper*	The Beatles	No. 1
Nowhere Man c/w *What Goes On?*	The Beatles	No. 1
Paperback Writer c/w *Rain*	The Beatles	No. 1
Yellow Submarine c/w *Eleanor Rigby*	The Beatles	No. 1
Penny Lane c/w *Strawberry Fields Forever*	The Beatles	No. 1
All You Need Is Love c/w *Baby You're A Rich Man*	The Beatles	No. 1

Hello, Goodbye c/w *I Am The Walrus*	The Beatles	No. 1
Lady Madonna c/w *The Inner Light*	The Beatles	No. 2
Hey Jude c/w *Revolution*	The Beatles	No. 1
The Ballad of John & Yoko c/w *Old Brown Shoe*	The Beatles	No. 7
Give Peace A Chance c/w *Remember Love*	Plastic Ono Band	No. 10
Something c/w *Come Together*	The Beatles	No. 1
Cold Turkey c/w *Don't Worry Kyoko*	Plastic Ono Band	No. 26
Instant Karma c/w *Who Has Seen The Wind*	John Ono Lennon	No. 3
Let It Be c/w *You Know My Name (Look Up The Number*	The Beatles	No. 1
The Long and Winding Road c/w *For You Blue*	The Beatles	No. 1
Beaucoups of Blues c/w *Coochy-Coochy*	Ringo Starr	No. 87
My Sweet Lord c/w *Isn't It A Pity*	George Harrison	No. 1
Mother c/w *Why*	John Lennon/Plastic Ono Band	No. 16
What Is Life? c/w *Apple Scruffs*	George Harrison	No. 10
Another Day c/w *Oh Woman Oh Why*	Paul McCartney	No. 5

Power To The People c/w *Touch Me*	John Lennon/ Plastic Ono Band	No. 8
It Don't Come Easy c/w *Early 1970*	Ringo Starr	No. 1
God Save Us c/w *Do The Oz*	Bill Elliott's Elastic Oz Band	No. 112
Bangla Desh c/w *Deep Blue*	George Harrison	No. 13
Uncle Albert/ *Admiral Halsey* c/w *Too Many People*	Paul and Linda McCartney	No. 1
Imagine c/w *It's So Hard*	John Lennon/Plastic Ono Band	No. 1
Happy Xmas (War Is *Over)* c/w *Listen, The Snow Is Falling*	John Lennon/ Plastic Ono Band	No. 28
Give Ireland Back To The Irish c/w *Give Ireland Back To The Irish* *(instrumental)*	Wings	No. 36
Back Off Boogaloo c/w *Blindman*	Ringo Starr	No. 8
Woman Is The Nigger Of the *World* c/w *Sisters O Sisters*	John Lennon/ Plastic Ono Band	No. 87
Mary Had A Little Lamb c/w *Little Woman Love*	Wings	No. 38
Hi, Hi, Hi c/w *C Moon*	Wings	No. 7
My Love c/w *The Mess*	Paul McCartney & Wings	No. 1
Give Me Love c/w *Miss O'Dell*	George Harrison	No. 1
Live and Let Die c/w *I Lie Around*	Wings	No. 1

Photograph c/w *Down And Out*	Ringo Starr	No. 1
Mind Games c/w *Meat City*	John Lennon	No. 10
Helen Wheels c/w *Country Dreamer*	Paul McCartney & Wings	No. 4
You're Sixteen c/w *Devil Woman*	Ringo Starr	No. 1
Jet c/w *Mamunia*	Paul McCartney & Wings	No. 5
Oh My My c/w *Step Lightly*	Ringo Starr	No. 5
Band On The Run c/w *Nineteen Hundred And Eight Five*	Paul McCartney & Wings	No. 1
Whatever Gets You Thru The Night c/w *Beef Jerky*	John Lennon	No. 1
Junior's Farm c/w *Sally G*	Paul McCartney & Wings	No. 5
Only You c/w *Call Me*	Ringo Starr	No. 9
Dark Horse c/w *I Don't Care Anymore*	George Harrison	No. 27
No. 9. Dream c/w *What You Got?*	John Lennon	No. 17
Ding Dong: Ding Dong c/w *Hari's On Tour (Express)*	George Harrison	No. 49
No No Song c/w *Snookeroo*	Ringo Starr	No. 5
Stand By Me c/w *Move Over Ms. L.*	John Lennon	No. 24
Listen To What The Man Said c/w *Love In Song*	Wings	No. 1

It's All Down To Goodnight *Vienna* c/w *Oo-wee*	Ringo Starr	No. 54
You c/w *World Of Stone*	George Harrison	No. 29
Letting Co c/w *You Gave Me The Answer*	Wings	No. 62
Venus And Mars c/w *Magneto and Titanium Man*	Wings	No. 28
Silly Love Songs c/w *Cook Of The House*	Wings	No. 1
Got To Get You Into My Life c/w *Helter Skelter*	The Beatles	No. 9
Let 'Em In c/w *Beware My Love*	Wings	No. 4
A Dose Of Rock 'n' Roll c/w *Cryin'*	Ringo Starr	No. 32
Ob-La-Di-Ob-La-Da c/w *Julia*	The Beatles	No. 75
This Song c/w *Learning How To Love You*	George Harrison	No. 33
Hey Baby c/w *Lady Gaye*	Ringo Starr	No. 93
Crackerbox Palace c/w *Learning How To Love You*	George Harrison	No. 26
Seaside Woman c/w *B-Side To Seaside*	Suzy and The Red Stripes	No. 92
Wings c/w *Just A Dream*	Ringo Starr	No. 119
Mull Of Kintyre c/w *Girl's School!*	Wings	No. 33
With A Little Luck c/w *Backwards Traveller/Cuff-Link*	Wings	No. 1

Lipstick Traces c/w *Old Time Relovin'*	Ringo Starr	No. 103
I've Had Enough c/w *Deliver Your Children*	Wings	No. 30

*Sgt. Pepper's Lonely Hearts
   Club Band* c/w
*With A Little Help From
   My Friends*
	The Beatles	No. 103

London Town c/w *I'm Carrying*	Wings	No. 48
Blow Away c/w *Soft Hearted Hana*	George Harrison	No. 17
Goodnight Tonight c/w *Daytime Nightime Suffering*	Wings	No. 7
Getting Closer c/w *Spin It On*	Wings	No. 22
Love Comes To Everyone c/w *Soft Touch*	George Harrison	No. 118
Arrow Through Me c/w *Old Siam, Sir*	Wings	No. 27
Coming Up c/w *Lunch Box Odd Sox*	Paul McCartney	No. 3
Waterfalls c/w *Check My Machine*	Paul McCartney	No. 83
(Just Like) Starting Over c/w *Kiss Kiss Kiss*	John Lennon	No. 1
Woman c/w *Beautiful Boys*	John Lennon	No. 2
Watching The Wheels c/w *Yes I'm Your Angel*	John Lennon	No. 9
All Those Years Ago c/w *Writing's On The Wall*	George Harrison	No. 3
Wrack My Brain c/w *Drumming Is My Madness*	Ringo Starr	No. 40

The Beatles Movie Medley	The Beatles	No. 39
Ebony and Ivory c/w *Rainclouds*	Paul McCartney	No. 40

ALBUMS

Meet The Beatles	The Beatles	No. 1
Introducing The Beatles	The Beatles	No. 1
The Beatles Second Album	The Beatles	No. 1
The American Tour With Ed Rudy	The Beatles	No. 32
A Hard Day's Night	The Beatles	No. 1
Something New	The Beatles	No. 2
Songs, Pictures And Stories Of The Fabulous Beatles	The Beatles	No. 79
The Beatles Story	The Beatles	No. 13
Beatles '65	The Beatles	No. 1
The Early Beatles	The Beatles	No. 29
Beatles VI	The Beatles	No. 1
Help!	The Beatles	No. 1
Rubber Soul	The Beatles	No. 1
Yesterday . . . And Today	The Beatles	No. 1
Revolver	The Beatles	No. 1
Sgt. Pepper's Lonely Hearts Club Band	The Beatles	No. 1
Magical Mystery Tour	The Beatles	No. 1
Unfinished Music No. I. Two Virgins	John & Yoko	No. 56
Abbey Road	The Beatles	No. 1
Wedding Album	John & Yoko	No. 108
Live Peace In Toronto: 1969	Plastic Ono Band	No. 18
Hey Jude (The Beatles Again)	The Beatles	No. 1
McCartney	Paul McCartney	No. 1
Sentimental Journey	Ringo Starr	No. 20
In The Beginning	The Beatles, featuring Tony Sheridan	No. 139
Let It Be	The Beatles	No. 1
Beaucoups Of Blues	Ringo Starr	No. 38
All Things Must Pass	George Harrison	No. 1
John Lennon/Plastic Ono Band	John Lennon	No. 2

Ram	Paul McCartney	No. 2
Imagine	John Lennon/Plastic Ono Band	No. 1
Wild Life	Wings	No. 9
Concert For Bangla Desh	George Harrison & Friends	No. 1
Sometime In New York City	John & Yoko/ Plastic Ono Band	No. 30
The Beatles 1962–1966	The Beatles	No. 4
The Beatles 1967–1970	The Beatles	No. 1
Red Rose Speedway	Paul McCartney & Wings	No. 1
Living In The Material World	George Harrison	No. 1
Live And Let Die: Title Track	Paul McCartney & Wings	No. 17
Ringo	Ringo Starr	No. 1
Mind Games	John Lennon	No. 6
Band On The Run	Paul McCartney & Wings	No. 1
Walls And Bridges	John Lennon	No. 1
Goodnight Vienna		
Dark Horse	George Harrison	No. 4
Rock 'n' Roll	John Lennon	No. 4
Venus & Mars	Wings	No. 1
Extra Texture	George Harrison	No. 9
Shaved Fish	John Lennon	No. 21
Blast From Your Past	Ringo Starr	No. 64
Wings At The Speed of Sound	Wings	No. 1
Rock 'n' Roll Music	The Beatles	No. 2
Ringo's Rotogravure	Ringo Starr	No. 45
The Best Of George Harrison	George Harrison	No. 33
Thirty Three And A $\frac{1}{3}$	George Harrison	No. 14
Wings Over America	Wings	No. 3
The Beatles At The Hollywood Bowl	The Beatles	No. 7
Live At The Star Club In Hamburg, Germany, 1962	The Beatles	No. 165
Ringo The 4th	Ringo Starr	No. 178
Love Songs	The Beatles	No. 36
London Town	Wings	No. 2
Bad Boy	Ringo Starr	No. 144
Wings Greatest	Wings	No. 23
George Harrison	George Harrison	No. 17

Back To The Egg	Wings	No. 7
Rarities	The Beatles	No. 26
McCartney II	Paul McCartney	No. 3
Rock 'n' Roll Music. Volume 1	The Beatles	No. 134
Rock 'n' Roll Music. Volume 2	The Beatles	No. 137
Double Fantasy	John Lennon & Yoko Ono	No. 1
The McCartney Interview	Paul McCartney	No. 141
Concerts For The People Of Kampuchea	Various Artists/ Paul McCartney & Wings	No. 31
Somewhere In England	George Harrison	No. 11
Stop And Smell The Roses	Ringo Starr	No. 78
Reel Music	The Beatles	No. 90

26 *Mersey Beat* Popularity Poll

The very first prize the Beatles were ever awarded was the *Mersey Beat* Shield, which I presented to them on behalf of the *Mersey Beat* newspaper. The publication only held a popularity poll twice. The first was in 1961 and the results were printed in January 1962. The second was printed in January 1963.

1961 POLL RESULTS

No. 1   The Beatles
No. 2   Gerry & The Pacemakers
No. 3   The Remo Four
No. 4   Rory Storm & The Hurricanes
No. 5   Johnny Sandon & The Searchers
No. 6   Kingsize Taylor & The Dominoes
No. 7   The Big Three
No. 8   The Strangers
No. 9   Faron & The Flamingos
No. 10   The Four Jays
No. 11   Ian & The Zodiacs
No. 12   The Undertakers
No. 13   Earl Preston & The T. T.'s
No. 14   Mark Peters & The Cyclones
No. 15   Karl Terry & The Cruisers
No. 16   Derry & The Seniors

No. 17   Steve & The Syndicate
No. 18   Dee Fenton & The Silhouettes
No. 19   Billy Kramer & The Coasters
No. 20   Dale Roberts & The Jaywalkers

1962 POLL RESULTS
No. 1   The Beatles
No. 2   Lee Curtis & The All Stars
No. 3   The Big Three (joint)
No. 3   Billy Kramer & The Coasters (joint)
No. 5   The Undertakers
No. 6   The Fourmost
No. 7   Gerry & The Pacemakers
No. 8   Johnny Sandon With The Remo Four
No. 9   Vic & The Spidermen
No. 10   The Mersey Beats
No. 11   The Swinging Blue Jeans
No. 12   The Strangers
No. 13   Group One
No. 14   Ian & The Zodiacs
No. 15   Pete MacLaine & The Dakotas
No. 16   The Dennisons
No. 17   Gus Travis & The Midnighters
No. 18   Mark Peters & The Cyclones
No. 19   Rory Storm & The Hurricanes
No. 20   Johnny Templar & The Hi-Cats

27 Birthday!

The Beatles, their families and friends: birthdates for every month of the year.

George Martin: 3rd January 1926 The Beatles' recording manager. An appointment he made to see Brian Epstein in 1962 was to completely transform his life.

Mike McCartney: 7th January 1944 Paul's younger brother, who made a successful career for himself as Mike McGear and had several hit records with his group, the Scaffold.

Happy Birthday, Mike. I promised I'd make him famous with this photograph.

Yoko Ono 18th February 1934 Born In Tokyo (her name means 'Ocean Child' in Japanese), she first met John Lennon at an exhibition of her works at the Indica Gallery in London.

George Harrison: 25th February 1943 The youngest member of the Beatles whose early career was under the Lennon/McCartney shadow, but emerged into the sunlight with *Something*.

Elton John: 25th March 1947 Godfather to Sean Lennon, Elton was a close friend of John and was joined by him on the stage of Madison Square Garden, leaving a record of the event for posterity.

James Taylor: 12th March 1948 Talented American/singer

songwriter who became the first signing to the Apple label.

Pattie Boyd: 17th March 1945 A pretty model who first met George on the set of *A Hard Day's Night* in which she had a small part, and later married her 'quiet Beatle'.

Eric Clapton: 30th March 1945 A leading guitarist who became the first rock musician to perform on a record with the Beatles when he played the guitar solo on *When My Guitar Softly Weeps*.

Jane Asher: 5th April 1946 Talented actress who, for 5 years, was Paul McCartney's sweetheart and the inspiration for several of his songs.

Julian Lennon: 8th April 1963 John's first son, generally neglected by John during his youth: the two began to get to know each other shortly before John's death.

Ravi Shankar: 7th April 1920 Master of the sitar, an Indian musical instrument in which George Harrison showed interest. After tuition by Ravi, George was able to use the sitar on a Western record for the first time.

Mary Hopkin: 3rd May 1950 Pretty blonde Welsh singer, recommended to Paul McCartney by Twiggy, who was to give Apple their first international hit with *Those Were The Days*.

Joe Cocker: 20th May 1944 Gruff-voiced singer from Sheffield who was to have a No. 1 hit record with *With A Little Help From My Friends*.

Bob Dylan: 24th May 1941 The major singer/songwriter of the Sixties who influenced and was influenced in turn by the Beatles.

Cilla Black: 27th May 1943 Brian Epstein's major female singing star and a friend of the Beatles from Liverpool who was to enjoy success for a further two decades and become one of Merseyside's most enduring stars.

Jimmy McCulloch: 4th June 1953 Talented guitarist who worked with Mike McGear on the *McGough & McGear* album and later became a member of Wings. He died in 1977.

Gordon Waller: 4th June 1945 One half of the Peter & Gordon duo who rose to fame on Lennon & McCartney's *World Without Love* and maintained their success for a short time on other John and Paul compositions and later fades without them.

Harry Nilsson: 15th June 1941 American singer, much

admired by the Beatles. John was to produce an album by him and Ringo made two films with him.

Paul McCartney: 18th June 1942 The member of the Beatles whose success after the break-up turned him into the world's highest paid musician.

Stuart Sutcliffe: 23rd June 1940 The group's original bass guitarist who died in 1962.

Ringo Starr: 7th July 1940 The eldest member of the Beatles and the last permanent member in the line-up.

James McCartney: 7th July 1902 Paul's father, a kindly man who passed away in 1976.

Peter Asher: 22nd July 1944 Brother of Jane Asher who enjoyed success with Peter & Gordon, recording Lennon & McCartney songs. He was to join Apple's recording division and later moved to the USA, where he became Linda Rondstadt's manager.

Mick Jagger: 26th July 1943 Leader of the Rolling Stones, the closest rivals to the Beatles during the sixties.

Dhani Harrison: 1st August 1978 George's first son, born in Windsor. Soon after Dhani was born, George married the mother, Olivia Arias, with whom he had been living for some time.

Maureen Cox: 4th August 1946 A Liverpool hairdresser, fan of the Beatles, who married her idol Ringo Starr.

Billy J. Kramer: 19th August 1943 Real name William Ashton, Billy was a Mersey singer who signed with Epstein and had a few major hits with Lennon & McCartney material.

Jason Starkey: 19th August 1967 Second son of Ringo and Maureen.

Keith Moon: 23rd August 1946 The madcap drummer with the Who and close friend of Ringo Starr and John Lennon. He died in 1978, after attending a party hosted by Paul McCartney in honour of Buddy Holly.

Mary McCartney: 28th August 1969 Paul and Linda's first child, named after Paul's mother.

Billy Preston: 9th September 1946 American singer/ keyboards player who backed the Beatles on the *Get Back* sessions. George Harrison produced his Apple single *That's The Way God Planned It*.

Cynthia Lennon: 10th September 1939 Blonde-haired art student, who married John Lennon and gave birth to his first son Julian.

Zak Starkey: 13th September 1965 Ringo and Maureen's first son who has followed in his father's drumbeats by becoming a drummer with a rock band.

James Louis McCartney: 12th September 1977 Paul and Linda's first son and third child.

Stella McCartney: 13th September 1971 Paul and Linda's second daughter.

Brian Epstein: 19th September 1934 The group's original manager who died, tragically, in 1967.

Linda McCartney: 24th September 1942 Daughter of a New York lawyer, Linda became a rock photographer and married Paul following a divorce from her first husband.

Richard Dilello: 28th September 1945 A press officer at Apple Records and author of the book *The Longest Cocktail Party*.

Sean Lennon: 9th October 1975 John and Yoko's first child and John's second son. A judicious sense of timing, arriving on John's own birthday.

John Lennon: 9th October 1949 Tragically murdered in 1980, when he was about to resume his career after a five-year spell caring for his son Sean.

Neil Aspinall: 13th October 1942 A fellow school chum of Paul and George when at The Liverpool Institute. Neil was the Beatles' original road manager and remained with them throughout their career.

Chuck Berry: 18th October 1931 One of the original Kings of Rock 'n' Roll. A seminal influence on the Beatles, who recorded several of his songs.

Denny Laine: 29th October 1944 A former member of the Moody Blues, this Birmingham-born singer/guitarist became a member of Wings on the invitation of Paul.

Lee Starkey: 17th November 1970 Third child and only daughter of Ringo's first marriage to Maureen.

Allen Klein: 18th December 1931 New York manager who the Beatles employed to look after their affairs on the recommendation of the Rolling Stones. Paul dissented and the Beatles break-up began.

Phil Spector: 25th December 1940 Celebrated American record producer whose association with the Beatles was probably not all that successful. Paul didn't like the result of his work on their master tapes and John wasn't too pleased with his work on a rock 'n' roll album.

Heather McCartney: 31st December 1963 Linda's daughter from her first marriage. Paul officially adopted her in 1969.

28 May I Introduce You?

Books for which Paul McCartney has written an Introduction. Initially, Paul started out with a very humorous piece for John's book, but subsequent requests didn't have the flair or humour

Paul's introductory notes for books have been getting smaller and smaller.

of that first piece and most are merely a few paragraphs of comment about the book or author.

In His Own Write by John Lennon. Paul contributes a full-page Introduction, penned in a style not unlike John's own, outlining their first meeting at Woolton village fête.

Linda's Pictures by Linda McCartney. The book describes Paul's contribution as a 'review.' It's actually two sentences long!

The Facts About A Pop Group: Featuring Wings by Dave Gelly. Seven lines of copy form Paul's introduction which briefly outlines what the book is about.

Paul McCartney: Composer/Artist Basically, a collection of the lyrics of Paul's songs, together with a series of his own illustrations. His introduction is once again short and merely describes the fact that he has provided the drawings.

Abbey Road by Brian Southall. A foreword rather than an introduction. Nine lines of copy in which he says he likes the Abbey Road Studios.

The Ocean View by Humphrey Ocean. A preface rather than an introduction. Nine lines of copy describing how Ocean was commissioned to capture a Wings' American tour in a series of paintings and drawings.

29 Luxembourg 20

In 1981, Radio Luxembourg ran a poll in which readers voted for their all-time favourite Beatles' numbers. They were:

No. 1 *Hey Jude*
No. 2 *She Loves You*
No. 3 *Yesterday*
No. 4 *Help!*
No. 5 *A Hard Day's Night*
No. 6 *Let It Be*
No. 7 *Can't Buy Me Love*
No. 8 *I Want To Hold Your Hand*
No. 9 *All My Loving*

No. 10   *Ticket To Ride*
No. 11   *Love Me Do*
No. 12   *Eleanor Rigby*
No. 13   *All You Need Is Love*
No. 14   *I Feel Fine*
No. 15   *Penny Lane*
No. 16   *Twist And Shout*
No. 17   *A Day In The Life*
No. 18   *Get Back*
No. 19   *Please Please Me*
No. 20   *Strawberry Fields Forever*

30 Sharing The Bill

The Beatles early Hamburg recordings were basically as a backing band to singer Tony Sheridan. The coupling was to be released and re-released from that time to this. But Sheridan wasn't the only act the Beatles had to share vinyl space with. Some enterprising American companies also teamed them up with other artists. Examples include:

Jolly What! The Beatles And Frank Ifield On Stage (Vee-Jay 1085)
This wasn't of course, recordings of a stage show, just various studio tracks put together by the label. Ironically, the Beatles and Frank Ifield did appear on stage together, at the Empire Theatre, Peterborough.
The Beatles vs. The Four Seasons (Vee-Jay DX-30)
Vee-Jay again, anxious to pad out what few Beatles tracks they had on their catalogue, paired them off with the Four Seasons on this gimmick, proclaiming: 'The International Battle Of The Century'.

The majority of bill-sharing exercises took place within the bootleg record field and the teamings there included:

Beatles vs. Chuck Berry
Beatles vs. Don Ho

Beatles vs. Buddy Holly and the Isley Brothers
Beatles vs. Little Richard and Larry Williams
Beatles vs. Carl Perkins
Best Of The Beatles and Jethro Tull
Dylan/Stones/Beatles
Elvis Meets . . . The Beatles

31 The Other Moptops

When Beatlemania hit the USA in February 1964, New York's radio station, WMCA, ran a competition for listeners to paint or draw someone in a Beatlewig – either celebrity pictures clipped from newspapers or photos of friends. The most popular subjects were:

Nikita Krushchev
Mayor Wagner
Alfred E. Newman (of *Mad* magazine)
Brigitte Bardot
The Jolly Green Giant

32 *Billboard* Charts

The American publication *Billboard* runs a 'Hot 100' chart of the best-selling singles in the USA. What follows are details of all the Beatles' positions in that chart until the group's eventual break-up.

I Want To Hold Your Hand Entered the charts on 18th January 1964 at No. 45, was No. 1 for 7 weeks with a chart life of 15 weeks.

She Loves You entered the charts on 25th January 1964 at No. 69 and was No. 1 for 2 weeks with a chart life of 15 weeks.

Please Please Me entered the charts on 1st February 1964 at No. 68 and eventually reached No. 3 with a chart life of 13 weeks.

I Saw Her Standing There entered the charts on 8th February

1964 at No. 68 and eventually reached No. 14 with a chart life of 11 weeks.

My Bonnie entered the charts on 15th February 1964 at No. 67 and eventually reached No. 26 with a chart life of 6 weeks.

From Me To You entered the charts on 7th March 1964 at No. 86 and eventually reached No. 41 with a chart life of 6 weeks.

Twist & Shout entered the charts on 14th March 1964 at No. 55 and eventually reached No. 2 with a chart life of 11 weeks.

Roll Over Beethoven entered the charts on 21st March 1964 at No. 79 and eventually reached No. 68 with a chart life of 4 weeks.

All My Loving entered the charts on 28th March 1964 at No. 71, eventually reaching No. 45 with a chart life of 6 weeks.

Do You Want To Know A Secret? entered the charts on 28th March 1964 at No. 78 and eventually reached No. 2 with a chart life of 11 weeks.

Can't Buy Me Love entered the charts on 28 March 1964 at No. 22, eventually reaching No. 1 for 5 weeks with a chart life of 10 weeks.

You Can't Do That entered the charts on 4th April 1964 at No. 65, eventually reaching No. 48 with a chart life of 4 weeks.

Thank You Girl entered the charts on 4th April 1964 at No. 79, eventually reaching No. 35 with a chart life of 7 weeks.

There's A Place entered the charts on 11th April 1964 for 1 week only at No. 74.

Love Me Do entered the charts on 11th April 1964 at No. 81, eventually reaching No. 1 for 1 week with a chart life of 14 weeks.

Why? entered the charts on 18th April 1964 at No. 88 for 1 week only.

P.S. I Love You entered the charts on 9th May 1964 at No. 64, eventually reaching No. 10 with a chart life of 3 weeks.

Four By The Beatles (EP) entered the charts on 13th June 1964 at No. 97, eventually reaching No. 92 with a chart life of 3 weeks.

Sie Liebt Dich entered the charts on 27th June 1964 for 1 week only at No. 97.

A Hard Day's Night entered the charts on 18th July 1964 at

No. 21, eventually reaching No. 1 for 2 weeks with a chart life of 13 weeks.

Ain't She Sweet entered the charts on 18th July 1964 at No. 90, eventually reaching No. 19 with a chart life of 9 weeks.

I Should Have Known Better entered the charts on 25th July 1964 at No. 75, eventually reaching No. 53 with a chart life of 4 weeks.

And I Love Her entered the charts on 25th July 1964 at No. 80, eventually reaching No. 12 with a chart life of 9 weeks.

If I Fell entered the charts on 1st August 1964 at No. 92, eventually reaching No. 53 with a chart life of 9 weeks.

I'll Cry Instead entered the charts on 1st August 1964 at No. 62, eventually reaching No. 25 with a chart life of 7 weeks.

I'm Happy Just To Dance With You entered the charts on 1st August 1964 for 1 week only at No. 95.

Matchbox entered the charts on 5th September 1964 at No. 81, eventually reaching No. 17 with a chart life of 8 weeks.

Slow Down entered the charts on 5th September 1964 at No. 99, eventually reaching No. 25 with a chart life of 7 weeks.

I Feel Fine entered the charts on 5th December 1964 at No. 22, eventually reaching No. 1 for 3 weeks with a chart life of 11 weeks.

She's A Woman entered the charts on 5th December 1964 at No. 46, eventually reaching No. 4 with a chart life of 9 weeks.

Eight Days A Week entered the charts on 20th February 1965 at No. 53, eventually reaching No. 1 for 2 weeks with a chart life of 10 weeks.

I Don't Want To Spoil The Party entered the charts on 20th February 1965 at No. 81, eventually reaching No. 39 with a chart life of 6 weeks.

Four By The Beatles (E.P). entered the charts on 27th February 1965 at No. 81, eventually reaching No. 68 with a chart life of 5 weeks.

Ticket to Ride entered the charts on 24th April 1965 at No. 59, eventually reaching No. 1 for 1 week with a chart life of 11 weeks.

Yes It Is entered the charts on 1st May 1965 at No. 71, eventually reaching No. 46 with a chart life of 4 weeks.

Help! entered the charts on 7th August 1965 at No. 42, even-

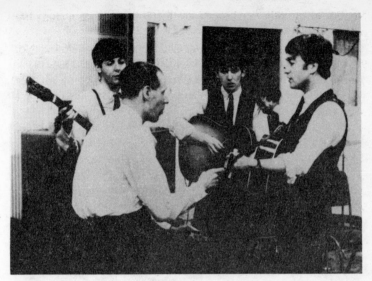

A musical combination which was to create record records.

tually reaching No. 1, for 3 weeks with a chart life of 13 weeks.

Yesterday entered the charts on 25th September 1965 at No. 45, eventually reaching No. 1 for 4 weeks with a chart life of 11 weeks.

Act Naturally entered the charts on 25th September 1965 at No. 87, eventually reaching No. 47 with a chart life of 7 weeks.

We Can Work It Out entered the charts on 18th December 1965 at No. 36, eventually reaching No. 1 for 3 weeks with a chart life of 10 weeks.

Day Tripper entered the charts on 18th December 1965 at No. 56, eventually reaching No. 5 with a chart life of 10 weeks.

Nowhere Man entered the charts on 5th March 1966 at No. 25, eventually reaching No. 3 with a chart life of 9 weeks.

What Goes On? entered the charts on 12th March 1966 at No. 89, moved to No. 81 the following week, then dropped out.

Paperback Writer entered the charts on 11th June 1966 at No. 28, eventually reached No. 1 for 2 weeks with a chart life of 10 weeks.

Rain entered the charts on 11th June 1966 at No. 72, eventually reaching No. 23 with a chart life of 7 weeks.

Yellow Submarine entered the charts on 20th August 1966 at No. 52, eventually reaching No. 2 with a chart life of 9 weeks.

Eleanor Rigby entered the charts on 27th August 1966 at No. 65, eventually reaching No. 11 with a chart life of 8 weeks.

Penny Lane entered the charts on 25th February 1967 at No. 85, eventually reaching No. 1 for 1 week with a chart life of 10 weeks.

Strawberry Fields Forever entered the charts on 25th February 1967 at No. 83, eventually reaching No. 8 with a chart life of 9 weeks.

All You Need Is Love entered the charts on 22nd July, 1967 at No. 71, eventually reaching No. 1 for 1 week with a chart life of 11 weeks.

Baby You're A Rich Man entered the charts on 29th July 1967 at No. 64, eventually reaching No. 34 with a chart life of 5 weeks.

Hello Goodbye entered the charts on 2nd December 1967 at No. 45, eventually reaching No. 1 for 3 weeks with a chart life of 11 weeks.

I Am The Walrus entered the charts on 9th December 1966 at No. 64, eventually reaching No. 56 with a chart life of 4 weeks.

Lady Madonna entered the charts on 23rd March 1968 at No. 23, eventually reaching No. 4 with a chart life of 11 weeks.

The Inner Light entered the charts on 30th March 1968 for 1 week only at No. 96.

Hey Jude entered the charts on 14th September 1968 at No. 10 eventually reaching No. 1 with a chart life of 19 weeks.

Revolution entered the charts on 14th September 1968 at No. 38, eventually reaching No. 12, with a chart life of 11 weeks.

Get Back entered the charts on 10th May 1969 at No. 10, eventually reaching No. 1 for 5 weeks with a chart life of 12 weeks.

Don't Let Me Down entered the charts on 10th May 1969 at No. 40, eventually reaching No. 35 with a chart life of 4 weeks.

The Ballad of John & Yoko entered the charts on 14th June 1969 at No. 71, eventually reaching No. 8, with a chart life of 9 weeks.

Come Together entered the charts on 18th October 1969 at No. 23 and after 6 weeks, during which it reached No. 2, it was tied in with the *Something* position for a further 10 weeks, reaching No. 1 for 1 week.

Something entered the charts on 18th October 1969 at No. 20 and, after 6 weeks, during which it reached No. 3, it was tied in with the *Come Together* position for a further 10 weeks, reaching No. 1 for 1 week.

Let It Be entered the charts on 21st March 1970 at No. 6, eventually reaching No. 1 for 2 weeks with a chart life of 14 weeks.

For You Blue/The Long & Winding Road entered the charts on 23rd May 1970 at No. 35, eventually reaching No. 1 for 2 weeks with a chart life of 10 weeks.

33 Pseudonyms

The first time the Beatles used pseudonyms was in 1960 on their short tour of Scotland. Paul called himself Paul Ramon, George called himself Carl Harrison and Stuart Sutcliffe adopted the name Stu De Stijl. It was reported that John called himself Johnny Silver, but he denied this. The Beatles rarely found the use of pseudonyms necessary during the sixties, although there were one or two examples, such as the time Paul called himself Bernard Webb, but the aliases appeared at the end of their career when they were recording or guesting on someone else's records and when John began travelling.

John, in particular, loved pseudonyms, which is not surprising from the author of *In His Own Write*, which indicates a love of ridiculous names. Some of the pseudonyms used by the members of the Beatles were as follows:

John Lennon
Mel Torment Used when he recorded the number *Scared*.
John O'Cean Used when he appeared on Yoko Ono's *Feeling The Space* album. The moniker is obviously inspired by the Japanese translation of Yoko's name 'Ocean Child'.

Dr Winston O'Boogie Used on the *Mind Games* album. Winston was his real middle name.

Mr. Winston O'Reggae Used on his number *Steel And Glass*.

Dr. Winston & Booker Table & The Maitre D's Another name which could have walked straight out of *In His Own Write*, obviously a pun inspired by Booker T & The M.G.'s. He used the name for his *Beef Jerky* single.

Reverend Thumbs Ghurkin Used on his *Old Dirt Road* song. One of the Ghurkin names.

Reverend Fred Ghurkin Another example of his fascination with the title 'Reverend', this time one of the pseudonyms on the *Walls & Bridges* album. He was also to use this name when he travelled abroad with Yoko, booking into some hotels as the Reverend Fred and Ada Ghurkin.

John Green One of the pseudonyms he used when travelling.

Paul McCartney
Paul didn't relish pseudonyms as much as John.

Bernard Webb He used this name when he penned the number *Woman* for Peter & Gordon, as he was interested in seeing how well a number of his would be received without using the magic McCartney name. He also used the alias *A. Smith* on the number

Apollo C. Vermouth Used when producing *I'm An Urban Spaceman* for the Bonzo Dog Doo Dah Band. Apollo is obviously linked with Spaceman because of the American Apollo missions.

Ringo Starr
R.S. Ringo was also a person who used pseudonyms sparingly. The few he did use were not so far removed from his own name, as with this example of his initials which he used for his appearance on David Hentschel's *Startling Music* album.

Ritchie Used for his contribution to Stephen Stills; *Stills* album.

Richie The first name by which he is known to friends – this time without the 't' – used by him on *The London Howling Wolf 'Sessions'* album.

Richie Snare Another thinly disguised alias, using his first name allied to 'snare', referring to drums. Anyone seeing that name on the *Son Of Schmilsson* album would soon guess the identity.

English Ritchie Another alias used on the *Stills* album.

Ognir Rats Simply the name Ringo Starr, spelled in reverse. A name used in his 1978 TV show *Ringo*, which adapted the Mark Twain classic *The Prince & The Pauper* to a contemporary setting in which there is a set of identical guys, one called Ringo Starr, the other Ognir Rats.

George Harrison
Next to John, George seemed to enjoy hiding under an alias, although his pseudonyms were nowhere near as colourful as John's.

Son Of Harry Used for his musical contribution to *It's Like You Never Left*, an album by Dave Mason.

P. Roducer George's alias on the album *Splinter*, a group he produced.

Hari Georgeson Used when he made a guest appearance on Billy Preston's *It's My Pleasure* album.

The George O'Hara-Smith Singers George's voice, overdubbed to produce the sound of several voices, which he used on his *All Things Must Pass* album.

Jai Raj Harisein Another of his pseudonyms on the *Splinter* album. A name with a touch of eastern promise!

George Harrysong Alias he used for his appearance on the *Son Of Schmilsson* album, similar to that of his early music publishing company 'Harrisongs Ltd'.

George O'Hara-Smith The Irish-sounding hyphenated name appears once again – on Ashton, Gardener & Dyke's *I'm Your Spiritual Breadman* album. The group had originally evolved from the Remo Four and George had promised to return the compliment when they recorded for him on the *Wonderwall* soundtrack.

George O'Hara A name he used thrice. As an alias on two of Garry Wright's albums: *Footprint* and *That Was Only Yesterday* and also on the Nicky Hopkins LP *The Tin Man Was A Dreamer*.

L'Angelo Mysterioso The alias used on the Cream's *Badge*

single, a song he co-wrote with Eric Clapton. He also used the name on Jack Bruce's album *Songs For A Tailor*.

34 Beatle Babes

There have been nine children who have resulted from the marriages of the four members of the Beatles. They are, in order of age:

Julian Lennon Born at Sefton General Hospital, Liverpool, on 8th April 1963. Son of John and Cynthia Lennon.

Zak Starkey Born at Queen Charlotte's Hospital, London, on 13th September 1965. Son of Maureen and Ringo Starr.

Jason Starkey Born at Queen Charlotte's Hospital, London, on 19th August 1967. Son of Maureen and Ringo Starr.

Mary McCartney Born at Queen Charlotte's Hospital, London, on 28th August 1969. The first daughter of Paul and Linda McCartney.

Lee Starkey Born at Queen Charlotte's Hospital, London, on 11th November 1970. Daughter of Maureen and Ringo Starr.

Stella McCartney Born at Queen Charlotte's Hospital, London, on 13th September 1971. Second daughter of Paul and Linda McCartney.

Sean Ono Lennon Born in New York Hospital, New York, on 9th October 1975. The only child of John and Yoko Lennon.

James Louis McCartney Born at Queen Charlotte's Hospital, London, on 12th September 1977. First son of Paul and Linda McCartney.

Dhani Harrison Born in Windsor, England, on 1st August 1979. First son of George and Olivia Harrison.

35 The *Melody Maker* Charts

The *Melody Maker* has been the longest-running British music weekly of them all. Here are the chart positions of the Beatles EPs and singles until the band broke up:

Love Me Do entered the charts on 27 November 1962 at

No. 48, eventually reaching No. 21 with a chart life of 16 weeks.

Please Please Me entered the charts on 19th January 1963 at No. 47 and eventually reached No. 1 for 2 weeks with a chart life of 18 weeks.

From Me To You entered the charts on 20th April 1963 at No. 19 and eventually reached No. 1 for 6 weeks, with a chart life of 20 weeks.

My Bonnie entered the charts on 15th June 1963 at No. 30, dropped to No. 46 the next week and left the chart.

Twist & Shout (EP) entered the charts on 27th July 1963 at No. 14 and eventually reached No. 2 with a chart life of 31 weeks.

She Loves You entered the charts on 31st August 1963 at No. 12 and eventually reached No. 1 for 5 weeks, with a chart life of 31 weeks.

The Beatles Hits (EP) entered the charts on 28th September 1963 at No. 44, eventually reaching No. 14 with a chart life of 12 weeks.

I Want To Hold Your Hand entered the charts on 7th December 1963 at No. 1 where it remained for 4 weeks, with a chart life of 18 weeks.

All My Loving (EP) entered the charts on 8th February 1964 at No. 42, eventually reaching No. 12 with a chart life of 12 weeks.

Can't Buy Me Love entered the charts on 28th March 1964 at No. 1 where it remained for 3 weeks with a chart life of 14 weeks.

Ain't She Sweet entered the chart on 13th June 1964 at No. 36, eventually reaching No. 24 with a chart life of 6 weeks.

Long Tall Sally (EP) entered the charts on 4th July 1964 at No. 20, eventually reaching No. 14 with a chart life of 13 weeks.

A Hard Day's Night entered the charts on 18th July 1964 at No. 1 where it remained for 4 weeks with a chart life of 15 weeks.

A Hard Day's Night (EP) entered the charts on 28th November 1964 at No. 48, reaching No. 34 with a chart life of 4 weeks.

I Feel Fine entered the charts on 5th December 1964 at No. 1 where it remained for 6 weeks with a chart life of 13 weeks.

Ticket to Ride entered the charts on 17th April 1965 at No. 1 where it remained for 5 weeks with a chart life of 12 weeks.

Help! entered the charts on 31st July 1965 at No. 1 where it remained for 4 weeks with a chart life of 13 weeks.

We Can Work It Out/Day Tripper entered the charts on 18th June 1966 at No. 1 where it remained for 4 weeks with a chart life of 10 weeks.

Yellow Submarine/Eleanor Rigby entered the charts on 13th August 1966 at No. 4, eventually reaching No. 1 for 3 weeks with a chart life of 12 weeks.

Penny Lane/Strawberry Fields Forever entered the charts on 25th February 1967 at No. 3, eventually reaching No. 1 for 3 weeks with a chart life of 10 weeks.

All You Need Is Love entered the charts on 15th July 1967 at No. 3, eventually reaching No. 1 for 3 weeks with a chart life of 11 weeks.

Hello Goodbye entered the charts on 2nd December 1967 at No. 3, eventually reaching No. 1 where it remained for 4 weeks with a chart life of 10 weeks.

Magical Mystery Tour (2 EPs) entered the charts on 16th December 1967 at No. 17, eventually reaching No. 1 for 1 week, with a chart life of 10 weeks.

Lady Madonna entered the charts on 23rd March 1968 at No. 3, eventually reaching No. 2 for 2 weeks with a chart life of 7 weeks.

Hey Jude entered the charts on 7th September 1968 at No. 1 where it remained for 4 weeks with a chart life of 13 weeks.

Get Back entered the charts on 26th April 1969 at No. 2, eventually reaching No. 1 for 5 weeks with a chart life of 13 weeks.

The Ballad Of John & Yoko entered the charts on 7th June 1969 at No. 15, eventually reaching No. 1 for 3 weeks with a chart life of 10 weeks.

Something entered the charts on 9th November 1969 at No. 26, eventually reaching No. 4 with a chart life of 10 weeks.

Let It Be entered the charts on 14th March 1970 at No. 15, eventually reaching No. 3 with a chart life of 8 weeks.

36 The Decca Audition Tracks

The Beatles travelled to London to record at Decca's West Hampstead Studios on 1st January 1962. Recording manager, Mike Smith, was quite impressed with the band, but his boss, Dick Rowe, eventually decided to sign up Brian Poole & The Tremeloes, who recorded the same day, rather than the Fab Four. It is generally assumed that they recorded fifteen tracks during the audition sessions and all of them have been available on bootleg recordings. They are:

1 *Like Dreamers Do*
2 *Till There Was You*
3 *The Sheik Of Araby*
4 *To Know Her Is To Love Her*
5 *Take Good Care Of My Baby*
6 *Memphis*
7 *Sure To Fall*
8 *Hello Little Girl*
9 *Three Cool Cats*
10 *Cryin', Waiting, Hoping*
11 *Love Of The Loved*
12 *September In The Rain*
13 *Besame Mucho*
14 *Searchin'*
15 *Money*

37 Tops At Abbey Road

One of the classic images of rock is the photograph of the Beatles walking across the zebra-crossing at Abbey Road. The street is in St. John's Wood, London, and houses the EMI recording studio which the Beatles popularized on their album *Abbey Road*. There had been a string of No. 1 hit records produced at Abbey Road since Eddie Calvert first hit the top spot with *Oh Mein Papa* in 1954. However, it was with the arrival of the Beatles and the Mersey sound that the studios became more popularly known. No. 1 records produced there in the sixties by Liverpool bands were:

The Beatles   *From Me To You* (1963)
Gerry & The Pacemakers *How Do You Do It?* (1963)
Gerry & The Pacemakers   *I Like It* (1963)
Billy J. Kramer & The Dakotas   *Bad To Me* (1963)
The Beatles   *She Loves You* (1963)
Gerry & The Pacemakers   *You'll Never Walk Alone* (1963)
The Beatles   *I Want To Hold Your Hand* (1963)
Cilla Black   *Anyone Who Had A Heart* (1964)
Billy J. Kramer   *Little Children* (1964)
The Beatles   *Can't Buy Me Love* (1964)
Cilla Black   *You're My World* (1964)
The Beatles   *A Hard Day's Night* (1964)
The Beatles   *I Feel Fine* (1964)
The Beatles   *Ticket To Ride* (1964)
The Beatles   *Help* (1965)
The Beatles   *Day Tripper/We Can Work It Out* (1965)
The Beatles   *Paperback Writer* (1966)
The Beatles   *Yellow Submarine/Eleanor Rigby* (1966)
The Beatles   *All You Need Is Love* (1967)
The Beatles   *Hello Goodbye* (1967)
The Beatles   *Lady Madonna* (1968)
The Beatles   *Hey Jude* (1968)
The Scaffold   *Lily The Pink* (1968)

During the seventies, there were only two Beatles-related No. 1s from the studios:

George Harrison *My Sweet Lord* (1971)
Wings *Mull Of Kintyre* (1977)

A complete list of every No. 1 hit from Abbey Road can be found in Brian Southall's book *Abbey Road*, published by Patrick Stephens Limited.

38 Mersey Beat 1984

The 28th January 1984 British chart had more Mersey acts in the Top 20 than at any time since the original Mersey wave in 1963. The positions were:

No. 1 *Relax* Frankie Goes To Hollywood
No. 2 *Pipes Of Peace* Paul McCartney
No. 3 *That's Living Alright* Joe Fagin
No. 6 *Nobody Told Me* John Lennon
No. 9 *Wishful Thinking* China Crisis
No. 17 *The Killing Moon* Echo & The Bunnymen
No. 19 *Love Is A Wonderful Colour* Icicle Works

John, Paul and Joe Fagin were all members of the original Mersey wave. Frankie Goes To Hollywood, China Crisis, Echo & The Bunnymen and Icicle Works, the new wave of Liverpool groups which also included such popular acts as Orchestral Manouvres In The Dark, Teardrop Explodes and Wah!

39 Mersey Beat Compilations

The very first albums to feature a selection of Mersey groups was Oriole's *This Is Mersey Beat*, Volumes One and Two, issued in 1963. Over the years, several other collections have been issued, most notably United Artists' *Mersey Beat '62–'64: The Sound Of Liverpool* (United Artists 305/6), on which I speak the Introduction; the thirty-six-track double album *Mersey Sound* (Decca DPA 3081/2), for which I wrote the sleeve notes; *Let's Stomp!: Liverpool Beat, 1963* (Edsel Ed 103), which Edsel Records issued in 1982, along with a series of albums by the Big Three, the Escorts, the Merseybeats and the Mojos. In 1983, the See For Miles label issued the twenty-track *Liverpool 1963 – 1968* album (CH 33), the first in a series. The most comprehensive album is *Mersey Beat* (PCSP 1783293), which I compiled for EMI Records. The double album was issued in October 1983. I'd originally selected forty tracks, but at the last minute there were contractual complications with three of the selections and we were unable to include *Money*, by Kingsize Taylor & The Dominoes; *Tricky Dicky* by Denny Seyton & The Sabres and a track by Liverpool's all-girl group The Liverbirds. The album was only available in the British Isles and the thirty-seven tracks were:

SIDE ONE

She Loves You   The Beatles
Sweets For My Sweet   The Searchers
The Hippy Hippy Shake   The Swinging Blue Jeans
Do You Love Me   Faron's Flamingos
Some Other Guy   The Big Three
I'm The One   Gerry & The Pacemakers
Just A Little Bit   The Undertakers
Bony Moronie   Howie Casey & The Seniors
Let's Stomp   Lee Curtis And The All Stars

SIDE TWO

Love Of The Loved   Cilla Black
Baby, I Need Your Loving   The Fourmost
Little Children   Billy J. Kramer
Ferry 'Cross The Mersey   Gerry & The Pacemakers
It's Love That Really Counts   The Merseybeats
I Know   Beryl Marsden
Wild Side Of Life   Tommy Quickly
Lies   Johnny Sandon & The Remo Four
Watch Your Step   Earl Preston & The T.T.'s

SIDE THREE

I Want To Hold Your Hand   The Beatles
Sugar And Spice   The Searchers
Good Golly Miss Molly   The Swinging Blue Jeans
Reelin' And A Rockin'   The Big Three
Bad To Me   Billy J. Kramer
Beechwood   Ian & The Zodiacs
Honey Don't   Rhythm & Blues Incorporated
The One To Cry   The Escorts
Ain't Nobody Like My Babe   The Dennisons
Everything's Alright   The Mojos

MERSEY BEAT

"The guitar's all right, John, but you'll never make a living out of it."
John Lennon's Aunt Mimi

MONO
2 Record Set

THE BEATLES ● THE SEARCHERS ● CILLA BLACK ● GERRY AND THE PACEMAKERS ● BILLY J. KRAMER ● THE KUBAS ● THE CHANTS
THE FOURMOST ● THE PETE BEST FOUR ● THE SWINGING BLUEJEANS ● FREDDIE STARR AND THE MIDNIGHTERS ● THE MERSEYBEATS
RORY STORM AND THE HURRICANES ● THE TRENDS ● JOHNNY SANDON AND THE REMO FOUR ● IAN AND THE ZODIACS ● ESCORTS
THE DENNISONS ● HOWIE CASEY AND THE SENIORS ● THE BIG THREE ● FARON'S FLAMINGOES ● LEE CURTIS AND THE ALL STARS
EARL ROYCE AND THE OLYMPICS ● THE MOJOS ● THE CRYIN SHAMES ● THE UNDERTAKERS ● RHYTHM AND BLUES INCORPORATED
BERYL MARSDEN ● EARL PRESTON AND THE T.T's ● THE DIMENSIONS ● TOMMY QUICKLY

PARLOPHONE   EMI

When I thought up the idea for the cover, I suggested that various members of Mersey Beat bands be included among the Cavern audience. Can you spot the faces?

SIDE FOUR

All My Loving   The Trends
Who Told You?   Freddie Starr & The Midnighters
A Thousand Stars   The Chants
America   Rory Storm & The Hurricanes
I'm Gonna Knock On Your Door   The Pete Best Four
Magic Potion   The Kubas
Please Stay   The Cryin' Shames
Tears On My Pillow   The Dimensions
Que Sera Sera   Earl Royce & The Olympics

81

40 BPI Jubilee Awards

In 1977, the year of the Queen's Silver Jubilee, The BPI (British Phonogram Industry) made some special awards covering the previous twenty-five years in the British music industry. The presentations were made at the Wembley Conference Centre on 18th October and awards included:

Best British Pop Album, 1952–1977: *Sgt. Pepper's Lonely Hearts Club Band* The Beatles
Best British Pop Group, 1952–1977: The Beatles
Best British Record Producer, 1952–1977: George Martin
Best British Pop Single, 1952–1977: *Bohemian Rhapsody* Queen (although the Beatles received a nomination for *She Loves You*)

41 Beatles Repertoire – 1

Spencer Leigh, author of *Let's All Go Down The Cavern*, was interviewing John Cochrane, a former member of Mersey band Wump & The Werbles, when John told him that he kept a list of the repertoires of various Mersey groups circa 1961 because, at the time, they didn't want to duplicate the tunes other groups were playing. He still retained a list of nineteen of the songs which the Beatles included in their on-stage repertoire during the early period. The songs the Beatles played were:

1   *C'mon Everybody*
2   *Twenty Flight Rock*
3   *Mean Woman Blues*
4   *Lucille*
5   *New Orleans*
6   *Crying, Waiting, Hoping*
7   *Mailman, Bring Me No More Blues*
8   *Hallelujah, I Love Her So*
9   *What'd I Say*
10 *Hey Good Lookin'*

11 *Blue Moon Of Kentucky*
12 *Love Me Tender*
13 *Red Sails In The Sunset*
14 *Over The Rainbow*
15 *Corrina, Corrina*
16 *Don't Forbid Me*
17 *Will You Still Love Me Tomorrow*
18 *Boys*
19 *Wooden Heart*

42 Beatles Repertoire – 2

Mike McCartney has collected a great deal of memorabilia over the years and in his book *Thank U Very Much*, he reproduced a list, penned by the Beatles, of one of their Cavern Club repertoires. The list reads:

1   Hippy
2   Shimmy
3   Red Hot
4   Besame
5   Rhythm & Blues
6   Open
7   Love Me Do
8   Postman
9   Picture
10 Feet's Too Big
11 Swingin' Thing
12 Fool of Somebody
13 Darktown
14 Baby It's You
15 Dream
16 P.S.
17 Money
18 Roll Over Beethoven
19 Long Tall Sally

The Beatles' own shorthand was clear enough to them, but

although I was present at virtually every Cavern gig they did, I can't translate the list fully. (1) is obviously Chan Romero's *Hippy Hippy Shake* with which they would often close their act. They never officially released a version of the number, although it is to be found on the Star Club recordings. The Beatles made their Cavern debut on a 'Swinging Blue Jeans Guest Night' and it was the Swinging Blue Jeans who had the major hit with this number. (2) This is possibly *Shimmy Shake*, the 1959 American single by Billy Land. (4) *Besame Mucho* , an 'oldie', which was revived by the Coasters in the fifties. There is no official Beatles' version on record, but as the group played it on various radio shows, it has turned up on a number of bootlegs. (5) If this list is from mid-1962, it could refer to Arthur Alexander's *A Shot Of Rhythm & Blues*, issued in March, 1962. (7) A Lennon & McCartney song which became their first single. (8) *Please Mr. Postman*, a rendition of the Marvellettes hit and one of several Motown numbers favoured by the Beatles. (10) *Your Feet's Too Big,* the Fab Four's rendition of the Fats Waller number. (12) Probably *If You Gotta Make A Fool Of Somebody*, which became a big hit for Manchester's Freddie & The Dreamers. (14) *Baby, It's You*, a hit for the Shirelles and a number which the group featured on their *Please Please Me* album. (16) *P. S. I Love You*, which became the flip side of their first single. (17) *Money*, another favourite, the Berry Gordy number which became Motown's first big hit. They featured the song on their *With The Beatles* album. (18) *Roll Over Beethoven*, Chuck Berry's rock 'n' roll classic. This is another number which emerged on the Star Club recordings. (19) *Long Tall Sally*, one of Paul's great rock performances. This Little Richard number was a highlight of their early act.

43 Characters – Real and Imagined

There could be a new definition of immortality: that of names which will live on in Beatles' songs. There are various characters mentioned in the numbers made famous by the Beatles, some of them real people. To those handful so honoured, their names will be sung, perhaps for centuries.

REAL CHARACTERS

Prudence (Farrow) (sister of actress Mia Farrow)	*Dear Prudence*
B. B. King (famous blues artist)	*Dig It*
Doris Day (famous blonde American film star)	*Dig It*
Matt Busby (Former manager of Manchester United FC)	*Dig It*
Georgie Wood (diminutive comedian)	*Dig It*
Jair Guru Deva (spiritual teacher)	*Across The Universe*
Peter Brown (best man at John and Yoko's wedding)	*The Ballad of John & Yoko*
Muddy Water(s) (a pun concerning the famous Blues artist)	*Come Together*
Elmore James (celebrated blues artist)	*For You Blue*
Paul (McCartney)	*Glass Onion*
Edgar Allan Poe (author of macabre stories)	*I Am The Walrus*
Julia (John's mother)	*Julia*
Mother Mary (Paul's mother)	*Mother Mary*
Martha (Paul's sheepdog)	*Martha My Dear*
Michelle (Howard) daughter of member of Beatles' staff)	*Michelle*
Chairman Mao (Communist leader of China)	*Revolution*
Mr (Harold) Wilson (former British Prime Minister, Labour Party)	*Taxman*

85

Mr (Edward) Heath (former British Prime Minister Conservative Party)	*Taxman*
Charles Hawtrey (probably the character actor from the *Carry On* films)	*Two Of Us*
(Bob) Dylan	*Yer Blues*
Ringo (Starr)	*You Know My Name*

IMAGINED CHARACTERS

Mr Kite	*For The Benefit Of Mr. Kite*
The Hendersons	*For The Benefit Of Mr. Kite*
Henry The Horse	*For The Benefit Of Mr. Kite*
Pablo Fanques	*For The Benefit Of Mr. Kite*
Bungalow Bill	*The Continuing Story Of Bungalow Bill*
The King of Marigold	*Cry Baby Cry*
The Duchess of Kirkcaldy	*Cry Baby Cry*
Dr. Robert	*Dr. Robert*
Eleanor Rigby	*Eleanor Rigby*
Father McKenzie	*Eleanor Rigby*
Jojo	*Get Back*
Loretta Martin	*Get Back*
Moretta Fart	*Get Back* (album version)
Lady Madonna	*Glass Onion/Lady Madonna*
Jude	*Hey Jude*
Rita	*Lovely Rita*
Lucy	*Lucy In The Sky With Diamonds*
Joan	*Maxwell's Silver Hammer*
Maxwell Edison	*Maxwell's Silver Hammer*
PC Thirty-One	*Maxwell's Silver Hammer*
Rose	*Maxwell's Silver Hammer*
Valerie	*Maxwell's Silver Hammer*
Mr Mustard	*Mean Mr. Mustard*
Pam	*Mean Mr. Mustard*
Desmond	*Ob-La-Di-Ob-La-Da*
Molly	*Ob-La-Di-Ob-La-Da*
Danny Boy	*One After 909*

Polythene Pam	*Polythene Pam*
Rocky Raccoon	*Rocky Raccoon*
Nancy (Lil) Magill	*Rocky Raccoon*
Dan	*Rocky Raccoon*
Sgt. Pepper	*Sgt. Pepper's Lonely Hearts Club Band*
Billy Shears	*Sgt. Pepper's Lonely Hearts Club Band*
Sadie	*Sexy Sadie*
Sun King	*Sun King*
Doris	*Two Of Us*
Vera	*When I'm Sixty Four*
Chuck	*When I'm Sixty Four*
Dave	*When I'm Sixty Four*
Mr. Bosun	*Yellow Submarine*
Mr. Jones	*Yer Blues*
Dennis O'Fell	*You Know My Name (Look Up The Number)*

Note: Captain Marvel appears in *The Continuing Story Of Bungalow Bill*. This is a reference to a famous comic cartoon character. 'Her Majesty' in *Her Majesty* is said to refer to Queen Elizabeth II, as this number is a tribute.

44 Beatle Methuselahs

Some Beatles' singles leapt straight into the No. 1 position, others had a relatively short chart life. The actual length of time a particular record spent in the charts did not necessarily indicate the volume of its sales. Here, in order, are the Beatles' records which had the lengthiest chart lives:

USA
1   *Hey Jude* (19 weeks)
2   *I Want To Hold Your Hand* (18 weeks)
3   *Love Me Do* (16 weeks)
4   *She Loves You* (16 weeks)
5   *Help!* (14 weeks)

6   *Come Together* (14 weeks)
7   *Twist & Shout* (13 weeks)
8   *Yesterday* (13 weeks)
9   *Something* (13 weeks)
10 *Let It Be* (13 weeks)

UK
1   *Twist & Shout* (EP) (32 weeks)
2   *She Loves You* (31 weeks)
3   *From Me To You* (21 weeks)
4   *I Want To Hold Your Hand* (21 weeks)
5   *Beatles Hits* (EP) (19 weeks)
6   *Love Me Do* (18 weeks)
7   *Please Please Me* (18 weeks)
8   *Get Back* (17 weeks)
9   *Hey Jude* (16 weeks)
10 *Can't Buy Me Love* (14 weeks)
11 *Help!* (14 weeks)

45 Rising Sons

In 1980, Japanese fan Tadahiko Kurio compiled a list of the top-selling Beatles' singles and albums in Japan. In order of sales, they were:

SINGLES
1   *Let It Be* (1,280,000)
2   *Hey Jude* (1,020,000)
3   *Rock and Roll Music* (840,000)
4   *Yesterday* (800,000)
5   *Come Together/Something* (780,000)
6   *Ob-La-Di-Ob-La-Da* (690,000)
7   *Get Back* (670,000)
8   *Help!* (560,000)
9   *I Want To Hold Your Hand* (520,000)
10 *Hello Goodbye* (480,000)

ALBUMS
1   *Let It Be* (1,230,000)
2   *Abbey Road* (1,080,000)
3   *Beatles 1962–1966* (750,000)
4   *A Collection Of Beatles Oldies* (720,000)
5   *Beatles 1967–1970* (700,000)
6   *Sgt. Pepper* (660,000)
7   *Help!* (520,000)
8   *Rubber Soul* (480,000)
9   *Hey Jude* (450,000)
10   *A Hard Day's Night* (440,000)

46 The British Tours 1960–1965

As the Silver Beatles, John, Paul, George, Stuart Sutcliffe and drummer Tommy Moore enjoyed a brief tour of Scotland in the Spring of 1960 as a backing band for singer Johnny Gentle. The Beatles' first real tour came about when agent Arthur Howes took an interest in the band. He'd booked them for a single appearance at the Embassy, Peterborough, on a bill with Frank Ifield to judge the audience reaction to the new band. It wasn't positive, but he decided to book them anyway and placed them on the bill of a Helen Shapiro tour. The Beatles were to enjoy six tours of Britain, plus a mini-tour.

Howes generally booked his tours into cinemas which were converted into theatres for the night. The pecking order of that first tour was: Helen Shapiro, Danny Williams, Kenny Lynch, The Beatles, The Kestrels, The Red Price Orchestra, The Honeys and compere Dave Allen. The tour began on 2nd February 1963 and the dates were:

2nd February   Bradford, Gaumont
3rd February   Doncaster, Gaumont
4th February   Bedford, Granada
7th February   Wakefield, Odeon
8th February   Carlisle, ABC
9th February   Sunderland, Empire Theatre
10th February   Peterborough, Embassy

23rd February	Mansfield, Granada
24th February	Coventry, Coventry Theatre
26th February	Taunton, Odeon
27th February	York, Rialto
28th February	Shrewsbury, Granada
1st March	Southport, Odeon
2nd March	Sheffield, City Hall
3rd March	Hanley, Gaumont

Within a week of that tour ending, they were on the road again, this time supporting the American artists, Tommy Roe and Chris Montez, who had recently enjoyed chart success in Britain. The rest of the bill comprised The Viscounts, Debbie Lee, Tony Marsh and The Terry Young Six. The dates were:

9th March	East Ham, Granada
10th March	Birmingham, Hippodrome
12th March	Bedford, Granada
13th March	York, Rialto
14th March	Wolverhampton, Gaumont
15th March	Bristol, Colston Hall
16th March	Sheffield City Hall
17th March	Peterborough, Embassy
18th March	Gloucester, ABC
19th March	Cambridge, ABC
20th March	Romford, Ritz
21st March	Croydon, ABC
22nd March	Doncaster, Gaumont
23rd March	Newcastle, City Hall
24th March	Liverpool, Empire
26th March	Mansfield, Granada
27th March	Northampton, ABC
28th March	Exeter, ABC
29th March	Lewisham, Odeon
30th March	Portsmouth, Guildhall
31st March	Leicester, De Montfort Hall

For their third British tour of 1963, they were billed above American singer Roy Orbison, whom Howes had originally booked as headliner. However, by that time, the Beatles were on such a crest of a wave that Howes asked Orbison to allow them to headline the tour. Gerry & The Pacemakers, their Liverpool stablemates, who had enjoyed a No. 1 success with *How Do You Do It?*, the number that the Beatles had turned down, were also on the bill, along with David Macbeth, Louise Cordet, Julie Grant, Ian Crawford, The Terry Young Six and Tony Marsh. The dates were:

18th	May	Slough, Granada
19th	May	Hanley, Gaumont
20th	May	Southampton, Gaumont
22nd	May	Ipswich, Gaumont
23rd	May	Nottingham, Odeon
24th	May	Walthamstow, Granada
25th	May	Sheffield, City Hall
26th	May	Liverpool, Empire
27th	May	Cardiff, Capitol
28th	May	Worcester, Gaumont
29th	May	York, Rialto
30th	May	Manchester, Odeon
31st	May	Southend, Odeon
1st	June	Tooting, Granada
2nd	June	Brighton, Hippodrome
3rd	June	Woolwich, Granada
4th	June	Birmingham, Town Hall
5th	June	Leeds, Odeon
7th	June	Glasgow, Odeon
8th	June	Newcastle, City Hall
9th	June	Blackburn, King George Hall.

Their fourth tour of the UK was preceded by a short mini-tour in which the support acts to the Beatles were singer Mike Berry and Liverpool band Freddie Starr & The Midnighters. The dates were:

4th September	Worcester, Gaumont
5th September	Taunton, Gaumont
6th September	Luton, Odeon

7th September   Croydon, Fairfield Hall
8th September   Blackpool, ABC

The Beatles continued to appear at several other concert halls and theatres in September and October, including a three-concert trip to Scotland, prior to their Swedish tour at the end of October. Their fourth British tour then commenced in November and they were supported by Peter Jay & The Jaywalkers, The Brook Brothers, The Vernons Girls, The Rhythm & Blues Quartet and Frank Berry. The dates were:

    1st November   Cheltenham, Gaumont
    2nd November   Sheffield, City Hall
    3rd November   Leeds, Odeon
    5th November   Slough, Adelphi
    6th November   Northampton, ABC
    7th November   Dublin, Ritz
    8th November   Belfast, Adelphi
    9th November   East Ham, Granada
   10th November   Birmingham, Hippodrome
   12th November   Portsmouth, Guild Hall
   13th November   Plymouth, ABC
   14th November   Exeter, ABC
   15th November   Bristol, Colston Hall
   16th November   Bournemouth, Winter Gardens
   17th November   Coventry, Coventry Theatre
   19th November   Wolverhampton, Gaumont
   20th November   Manchester, Ardwick Apollo
   21st November   Carlisle, ABC
   22nd November   Stockton, Globe
   23rd November   Newcastle, City Hall
   24th November   Hull, ABC
   26th November   Cambridge, ABC
   27th November   York, Rialto
   28th November   Lincoln, ABC
   29th November   Huddersfield, ABC
   30th November   Sunderland, Empire
    1st December   Leicester, De Montfort Hall
    8th December   Lewisham, Odeon

9th December	Southend, Odeon
10th December	Doncaster, Gaumont
11th December	Scarborough, Futurist
12th December	Nottingham, Odeon
13th December	Southampton, Gaumont

The fourth tour was to be the longest UK one. The next British tour began in October 1964, following a world tour and an American tour. Their support acts were American singer Mary Wells, Liverpool stablemates Tommy Quickly and the Remo Four, and Brian Epstein discoveries Michael Haslam and The Rusticks. The bill was completed by compere Bob Bain and the instrumental band Sounds Incorporated. The dates were:

9th October	Bradford, Gaumont
10th October	Leicester, De Montfort Hall
13th October	Wigan, ABC
14th October	Ardwick, Apollo
15th October	Stockton, Globe
16th October	Hull, ABC
19th October	Edinburgh, ABC
20th October	Dundee, Caird Hall
21st October	Glasgow, Odeon
22nd October	Leeds, Odeon
23rd October	London, Kilburn, Gaumont State
24th October	Walthamstow, Granada
25th October	Brighton, Hippodrome
28th October	Exeter, ABC
29th October	Plymouth, ABC
1st November	Finsbury Park, Astoria
2nd November	Belfast, Ritz
4th November	Luton, Ritz
5th November	Nottingham, Odeon
6th November	Southampton, Gaumont
7th November	Cardiff, Capitol
8th November	Liverpool, Empire
9th November	Sheffield, City Hall
10th November	Bristol, Colston Hall

Their sixth and final tour of the UK took place in December 1965 and was fairly brief. Their support acts included the Moody Blues, Liverpool band the Koobas, Liverpool singers Beryl Marsden and Steve Aldo and Southend band the Paramounts, who were to evolve into Procol Harum. Their dates were:

3rd December	Glasgow, Odeon
4th December	Newcastle, City Hall
5th December	Liverpool, Empire
7th December	Manchester, Ardwick, Apollo
8th December	Sheffield, City Hall
9th December	Birmingham, Odeon
10th December	London, Hammersmith Odeon
11th December	London, Finsbury Park Astoria
12th December	Cardiff, Capitol

47 The American Tours 1964–1966

The Beatles only toured the USA three times in their career. The first tour lasted 5 weeks, the last less than 3. They first appeared in the USA in February 1964 for some television appearances on *The Ed Sullivan Show*, but they also made two live concert appearances:

11th February	Washington DC, Washington Coliseum
12th February	New York, Carnegie Hall

They returned to the USA later that year for their first major tour. The acts on the bill included Jackie De Shannon, The Righteous Brothers, the Bill Black Combo and the Exciters. The dates were:

19th August	San Francisco, Cow Palace
20th August	Las Vegas, Convention Hall
21st August	Seattle, Municipal Stadium

22nd August	Vancouver, Empire Stadium
23rd August	Los Angeles, Hollywood Bowl
26th August	Denver, Red Rock Stadium
27th August	Cincinnati, the Gardens
28th August	New York, Forest Hills Stadium
30th August	Atlantic City, Convention Hall
2nd September	Philadelphia, Concert Hall
3rd September	Indianapolis, State Fair Coliseum
4th September	Milwaukee, Auditorium
5th September	Chicago, International Amphitheatre
6th September	Detroit, Olympic Stadium
7th September	Toronto, Maple Leaf Gardens
8th September	Montreal, Forum
11th September	Jacksonville, Gator Bowl
12th September	Boston, Boston Gardens
13th September	Baltimore, Civic Centre

Their second tour of the USA in 1965 was their shortest one and comprised only a dozen appearances. They were supported by the King Curtis Band, Cannibal & The Headhunters, Brenda Holloway and Sounds Incorporated. The dates were:

15th August	New York, Shea Stadium
16th August	New York, Shea Stadium
17th August	Toronto, Maple Leaf Stadium
18th August	Atlanta, Atlanta Stadium
19th August	Houston, Sam Houston Coliseum
20th August	Chicago Comiskey Park
21st August	Minneapolis, Metropolitan Stadium
22nd August	Portland, Portland Coliseum
28th August	San Diego, Balboa Stadium
29th August	Los Angeles, Hollywood Bowl
30th August	Los Angeles, Hollywood Bowl
31st August	San Francisco, Cow Palace

Their August 1966 American tour was the last tour of their career. They were supported by the Ronettes and Cyrkle. The dates were:

12th August	Chicago, International Amphitheater
13th August	Detroit, Olympic Stadium
14th August	Cleveland, Municipal Stadium
15th August	Washington DC, Washington Stadium
16th August	Philadelphia, Philadelphia Stadium
17th August	Toronto, Maple Leaf Gardens
18th August	Boston, Suffolk Downs Racetrack
19th August	Memphis, Memphis Coliseum
20th August	Cincinnati, Crosley Field
21st August	St. Louis, Busch Stadium
23rd August	New York, Shea Stadium
24th August	New York, Shea Stadium
25th August	Seattle, Seattle Coliseum
28th August	Los Angeles, Dodger Stadium
29th August	San Francisco, Candlestick Park

48 The Beatles in Europe 1963–1966

The Beatles' first European concert stint was a short tour of Sweden in 1963 between 24th October and 29th October. Full dates were:

24th October	Stockholm, Karaplan
25th October	Karlstadt
26th October	Stockholm, Kungliga Tennishallen
27th October	Gothenburg
28th October	Boras
29th October	Eskilstuna

Their next Continental foray took place the following year, in 1964, when they appeared for 3 weeks at the Olympia Theatre, Paris, commencing 16th January on a bill with Trini Lopez and Sylvie Vartan. Later that year, they preceded their tour of Hong Kong and Australasia by some concerts in Denmark on:

The Fab Four – raring to go.

4th June   Copenhagen, KB Hall
6th June   Blokker, Exhibition Hall

Their first major European tour took place in 1965. The dates were:

20th June Paris, Palais des Sports
22nd June Lyons, Palais d'Hiver
24th June Milan, Velodromo Vigonelli
26th June Genoa, Palais des Sports
27th June Rome, Adriana Hotel
30th June Nice, Palais des Fetes
 2nd July Madrid, Plaza De Toros Monumental
 3rd July Barcelona, Plaza De Toros

Their final Continental concerts took place in Germany in 1966, appropriately in the European country where they performed regularly early in their career in Hamburg clubs. There were three dates:

24th June   Munich, Circus Krone
25th June   Essen, Grughalle
26th June   Hamburg, Ernst Merck Halle

49 George On Tour In Seventy-Four

Following the demise of the Beatles, George made some appearances in 1969 with Eric Clapton and Delaney & Bonnie & Friends, including one at the famous Lyceum Ballroom, the Strand, London, on 15th December which was billed as John Lennon & The Plastic Ono Supergroup and recorded for use in John's double album *Sometime In New York City*. A highlight for George was his *Concert For Bangla Desh* at the Madison Square Garden on 1st August 1971. His first major tour since leaving the Beatles took place at the end of 1974. His backing band comprised Billy Preston (keyboards), Robben Ford (guitar), Willie Weeks (bass), Andy Newmark (Drums), Tom Scott (saxes/woodwind), Emile Rochards (Percussion) and Chuck Findley (trumpet/trombone). Also on the bill was Indian musician Ravi Shankar. The tour dates were as follows:

2nd November	Vancouver, Pacific Coliseum
4th November	Seattle, Seattle Centre, Coliseum
7th November	San Francisco, Cow Palace
8th November	Oakland, Coliseum
10th November	Long Beach, Arena
11th November	Los Angeles, Forum
12th November	Los Angeles, Forum
14th November	Phoenix
16th November	Salt Lake City, Salt Palace
18th November	Denver, Coliseum
20th November	St. Louis, Arena
21st November	Tulsa, Civic Centre
22nd November	Fort Worth
24th November	Houston, Hofheinz Pavilion
26th November	Baton Rouge, LSU Assembly Centre

27th	November	Memphis, Mid-South Coliseum
28th	November	Atlanta, Omni
30th	November	Chicago, Stadium
2nd	December	Cleveland, Coliseum
4th	December	Detroit, Olympia Stadium
6th	December	Toronto, Maple Leaf Gardens
8th	December	Montreal, Forum
10th	December	Boston, Boston Gardens
11th	December	Providence, Civic Center
13th	December	Washington DC, Capitol Center
15th	December	Long Island, Nassau Coliseum
16th	December	Philadelphia, Spectrum
17th	December	Philadelphia, Spectrum
19th	December	New York, Madison Square Garden
20th	December	New York, Madison Square Garden

50 Wings Over The World
1972–1976

Paul McCartney's Wings, whose basic three members (Paul, Linda McCartney, Denny Laine) were joined by various musicians over a period of years, embarked on several tours following their debut at Nottingham University in 1972 when the line-up was: Paul McCartney (bass/vocals), Linda McCartney (keyboards), Denny Laine (guitar), Henry McCullough (guitar) and Denny Seiwell (drums). Between 9th and 23rd February, they appeared at the following British centres of learning:

9th	February	Nottingham University
10th	February	York University
11th	February	Hull University
13th	February	Newcastle University
14th	February	Lancaster University
16th	February	Leeds Town Hall
17th	February	Sheffield University
18th	February	University of Manchester, Salford
21st	February	Birmingham University

22nd February   Swansea University
23rd February   Oxford University

The group continued to tour during 1972 by embarking on a series of major appearances in Europe thoughout July and August. The tour commenced in France.

9th   July   Chateau Vallon, France, Centre Culturelle
12th   July   Juan Les Pins, France
13th   July   Arles, France, Theatre Antique
14th   July   Lyon, France
16th   July   Paris, France, Olympia
18th   July   Munich, Germany, Circus Krone
19th   July   Frankfurt, Germany, Offenbach Hall
21st   July   Zurich, Switzerland Congress Halle
22nd   July   Montreaux, Switzerland, Pavilion
1st   August   Copenhagen, Denmark, KB Hall
4th   August   Helsinki, Finland, Maess Hall
5th   August   Turku, Finland, Indraets
7th   August   Stockholm, Sweden, Tivoli Gardens
8th   August   Örebro, Sweden, Idretis Hall
9th   August   Olso, Norway
10th   August   Gothenburg, Sweden, Scandinavian Halle
11th   August   Lund, Sweden, Olympean
13th   August   Odense, Denmark, Flyns Farum
14th   August   Århus, Denmark, Vejlby Risskov Hallen
16th   August   Hanover, Germany
17th   August   Groningen, Holland, Evenementenhal
18th   August   Rotterdam, Holland, Doelen
19th   August   Breda, Holland, Turschip
20th   August   Amsterdam, Holland, Concert Gerbou
21st   August   The Hague, Holland, Congresgebouw
22nd   August   Brussels, Belgium, Circus Royale
24th   August   Berlin, Germany, Deutschland Halle

The group next performed at a gig at the Hard Rock Café in London on 18th March 1973, prior to their British tour almost 2 months later. The dates were:

11th	May	Birmingham, Hippodrome
12th	May	Oxford, New Theatre
13th	May	Cardiff, Capitol Theatre
15th	May	Bournemouth, Winter Gardens
16th	May	Manchester, Hard Rock
17th	May	Manchester, Hard Rock
18th	May	Liverpool, Empire
19th	May	Leeds University
21st	May	Preston, Guildhall
22nd	May	Edinburgh, Odeon
23rd	May	Edinburgh, Odeon
24th	May	Glasgow, Greens Playhouse
25th	May	Hammersmith, London, Odeon
26th	May	Hammersmith, London, Odeon
27th	May	Hammersmith, London, Odeon
4th	July	Sheffield, City Hall
6th	July	Birmingham, Odeon
9th	July	Leicester, Odeon
10th	July	Newcastle, City Hall

In 1975, they toured the UK again, followed by a short tour of Australia. Their line-up was now: Paul McCartney (bass guitar), Linda McCartney (keyboards), Denny Laine (guitar), Jimmy McCulloch (guitar) and Joe English (drums). They also took a four-piece horn section on tour with them comprising: Howie Casey (saxophone), Tony Dorsey (trombone), Steve Howard (trumpet, flugelhorn) and Thadeus Richard (saxophone). Their British dates were:

9th September	Southampton, Gaumont
10th September	Bristol, Hippodrome
11th September	Cardiff, Capitol Theatre
12th September	Manchester, Free Trade Hall
13th September	Birmingham, Hippodrome,
15th September	Liverpool, Empire Theatre
16th September	Newcastle, City Hall
17th September	Hammersmith, London, Odeon
18th September	Hammersmith, London, Odeon
20th September	Edinburgh, Usher Hall

| 21st September | Glasgow, Apollo Theatre |
| 23rd September | Dundee, Caird Hall |

Their Australian tour followed after a pause of 1 month:

1st November	Perth, Entertainment Centre
4th November	Adelaide, Apollo Stadium
5th November	Adelaide, Apollo Stadium
7th November	Sydney, Horden Pavilion
8th November	Sydney, Horden Pavilion
10th November	Brisbane, Festival Hall
11th November	Brisbane, Festival Hall
13th November	Melbourne, Myer Music Bowl
14th November	Melbourne, Myer Music Bowl

1976 also proved to be a busy touring year for Wings as they appeared on two mini-European tours, sandwiching their first tour of the USA. Their initial European dates were:

20th March	Copenhagen, Denmark, Falkoner Theatre
21st March	Copenhagen, Denmark, Falkoner Theatre
23rd March	Berlin, Germany, Deutschland Halle
25th March	Rotterdam, Holland, Ahoy Sports Stadium
26th March	Paris, France, Pavilion

They then embarked on a lengthy tour of the USA:

3rd May	Fort Worth TCCC (Tarrant County Convention)
4th May	Houston, Summit
7th May	Detroit, Olympia
8th May	Detroit, Olympia
9th May	Toronto, Canada, Maple Leaf Gardens
10th May	Cleveland, Richfield Coliseum
12th May	Philadelphia, Spectrum Bowl
14th May	Philadelphia, Spectrum Bowl
15th May	Washington DC, Capitol Centre
16th May	Washington DC, Capitol Centre
18th May	Atlanta, Omni
19th May	Atlanta, Omni

21st	May	Long Island, Nassau Coliseum
22nd	May	Boston, Boston Gardens
24th	May	New York, Madison Square Garden
27th	May	Cincinnati, River Front Stadium
29th	May	Kansas City, Kemper Arena
31st	May	Chicago, Chicago Stadium
1st	June	Chicago, Chicago Stadium
2nd	June	Chicago, Chicago Stadium
4th	June	St. Paul, Civic Centre
7th	June	Denver, McNichols Arena
10th	June	Seattle, King Dome
13th	June	San Francisco, Cow Palace
14th	June	San Francisco, Cow Palace
16th	June	San Diego, Sports Arena
18th	June	Tucson, Community centre
21st	June	Los Angeles, Forum
22nd	June	Los Angeles, Forum
23rd	June	Los Angeles, Forum

Later in the year, Wings returned to Europe for a short tour:

19th	September	Vienna, Austria, Stadthalle
21st	September	Zagreb, Yugoslavia, Dom Sportova
25th	September	Venice, Italy, Plaza San Marco
27th	September	Munich, Germany, Olympiahalle

They finished off the year with concerts at the Empire Pool, Wembley, London on 19th, 20th and 21st October.

51 Beatle Guide Books

I wrote a two-part feature *The Beatles Liverpool Days* for *Beatles Monthly* in the issues dated September and October 1978, which were the first articles to describe the Beatles' haunts in Liverpool. They proved so popular that, in August 1979, *Beatles Monthly* printed my feature *The Beatles' Liverpool*, subtitled *A Guide To All The Places Associated With John, Paul, George And Ringo*. The feature traced all their places of birth,

A weekend on the Mersey? In 1984, nearly three million visitors found it quite enjoyable!

homes, schools and the venues where the Beatles performed in Liverpool. I also introduced a *Beatle Walk*, a guide to the city centre, describing the places of interest with a Beatles' association. This also proved popular, so I compiled *The Beatles' London*, a two-part series which apppeared in the January and February 1980 issue of *Beatles Monthly*. Part One concentrated on their radio, television, stage and recording venues and Part Two was a more personal look at their homes, offices, the clubs they frequented and so on. I also included a London almanac.

The basic idea has been successfully adapted in book form on a number of occasions and the Beatles' guidebooks include:

In The Footsteps Of The Beatles By Mike Evans and Ron Jones, first published in a limited edition by Merseyside County Council in 1981. This is probably the best guide to Liverpool itself, with lots of photos, many of which originally appeared in *Mersey Beat*.

Lots Of Liverpool By the staff of the fanzine *Beatles Unlimited*. Published in 1982, this is an exhaustive guide to the entire Merseyside area, with lots of illustrations.

The Beatles' England By David Bacon and Norman Maslov. Published by Columbus Books in 1982. This is the most lavish of the guide books, with more photographs than text, covering London, Liverpool, Hamburg and other places of interest.

Follow The Merseybeat Road By Sam Leach, published by

Eden Publications in 1983, is a guide to the Merseyside area with lots of illustrations and anecdotes circa 1962/3.

Beatlefan The major American fanzine ran *The Beatles London Town – A Tour* in their Issue No. 4 of Volume 2 and *Liverpool: The Beatles' Trail* in their Issue No. 6 of Volume 2.

52 Provincial Poll

In 1982, the provincial newspaper the *Hull Daily Mail* held a readers' poll to discover the ten most popular Beatles' singles. Their readers voted for the following, in order:

1 *She Loves You*
2 *Yesterday*
3 *Hey Jude*
4 *Help!*
5 *I Want To Hold Your Hand*
6 *A Hard Day's Night*
7 *Let It Be*
8 *All You Need Is Love*
9 *Can't Buy Me Love*
10 *Get Back*

53 The RIAA Discs

The Recording Industry of America (RIAA) is an organisation which was launched on 14th March 1958 with the aim of auditing sales of million-selling singles in the USA. It also audits the sales of albums which top the 500,000 mark. The RIAA present Gold Discs to artists who have achieved these figures with sales of their singles and albums and the Beatles have won more RIAA awards than any other act – a total of forty-two. Paul McCartney, both as a solo artist and leader of Wings, has received a further sixteen awards.

Here is a list of the Gold Discs awards awarded to the Beatles and to the solo recordings of the individual members and also the dates on which they were officially recognised. The list details awards until the end of the seventies and singles are indicated by the sign (s).

3rd February 1964	*Meet The Beatles*
	I Want To Hold Your Hand (s)
31st March 1964	*Can't Buy Me Love* (s)
13th April 1964	*The Beatles Second Album*
24th August 1964	*Something New*
25th August 1964	*A Hard Day's Night* (s)
31st December 1964	*Beatles '65*
	The Beatles Story
	I Feel Fine (s)
1st July 1965	*Beatles VI*
23rd August 1965	*Help!*
2nd September 1965	*Help!* (s)
16th September 1965	*Eight Days A Week* (s)
20th October 1965	*Yesterday* (s)
24th December 1965	*Rubber Soul*
6th January 1966	*We Can Work It Out* (s)
1st April 1966	*Nowhere Man* (s)
8th July 1966	*Yesterday & Today*
14th July 1966	*Paperback Writer* (s)
22nd August 1966	*Revolver*
12th September 1966	*Yellow Submarine* (s)
20th March 1967	*Penny Lane* (s)
15th June 1967	*Sgt. Pepper's Lonely Hearts Club Band*
11th September 1967	*All You Need Is Love* (s)
15th December 1967	*Magical Mystery Tour*
	Hello Goodbye (s)
8th April 1968	*Lady Madonna* (s)
13th September 1968	*Hey Jude* (s)
6th December 1968	*The Beatles*
5th February 1969	*Yellow Submarine*
19th May 1969	*Get Back* (s)
16th July 1969	*The Ballad of John & Yoko* (s)
	The Beatles
27th October 1969	*Abbey Road*
	Something (s)

6th March 1970	*Hey Jude*
17th March 1970	*Plastic Ono Band Live Peace In Toronto*
	Let It Be (s) Plastic Ono Band
30th April 1970	*McCartney*
26th May 1970	*Let It Be*
14th December 1970	*Instant Karma* John Lennon (s)
	My Sweet Lord George Harrison (s)
17th December 1970	*All Things Must Pass* George Harrison
28th January 1971	*Plastic Ono Band*
9th June 1971	*Ram* Paul & Linda McCartney
3rd August 1971	*It Don't Come Easy* Ringo Starr (s)
21st September 1971	*Uncle Albert/Admiral Halsey* Paul & Linda McCartney (s)
1st October 1971	*Imagine* John Lennon
4th January 1972	*Concert For Bangla Desh* George Harrison & Friends
13th January 1973	*Wildlife* Wings
13th April 1973	*The Beatles 1962–1966*
	The Beatles 1966–1970
25th May 1973	*Red Rose Speedway* Paul McCartney & Wings
1st June 1973	*Living In The Material World* George Harrison
6th July 1973	*My Love* Paul McCartney & Wings
31st August 1973	*Live & Let Die* Paul McCartney & Wings (s)
8th November 1973	*Ringo* Ringo Starr
30th November 1973	*Mind Games* John Lennon
7th December 1973	*Band On The Run* Paul McCartney & Wings
28th December 1973	*Photograph* Ringo Starr
8th January 1974	*The Early Beatles*
31st January 1974	*You're Sixteen* Ringo Starr (s)
4th June 1974	*Band On The Run* Paul McCartney & Wings (s)
22nd October 1974	*Walls & Bridges* John Lennon

9th December 1974	*Goodnight Vienna* Ringo Starr
16th December 1974	*Dark Horse* George Harrison
5th September 1975	*Listen To What The Man Said* Paul McCartney & Wings (s)
11th November 1975	*Extra Texture* George Harrison
25th March 1976	*Wings At The Speed Of Sound* Paul McCartney & Wings
11th June 1976	*Silly Love Songs* Paul McCartney & Wings (s)
14th June 1976	*Rock 'n' Roll Music* The Beatles
25th October 1976	*Let 'Em In* Paul McCartney & Wings (s)
19th January 1977	*Thirty Three & A ⅓* George Harrison
15th February 1977	*The Best Of George Harrison* George Harrison
5th May 1977	*The Beatles At The Hollywood Bowl*
24th October 1977	*Love Songs*
30th March 1978	*London Town* Paul McCartney & Wings
8th May 1979	*George Harrison* George Harrison
18th June 1979	*Back To The Egg* Wings

The RIAA introduced Platinum Disc awards in 1976 and the Beatles have relatively few, despite the fact that combined sales of their records since the original Gold Disc awards would doubtless have merited many. The RIAA refuses to grant Platinum Discs for records produced before their introduction in 1976.

The Platinum Discs awarded from 1976 until the end of 1978 were:

3rd May 1976	*Wings At The Speed Of Sound* Wings
14th June 1976	*Rock 'n' Roll Music* The Beatles
20th December 1976	*Wings Over America* Wings
12th August 1977	*Beatles At The Hollywood Bowl* The Beatles

30th March 1978	*London Town* Wings
18th June 1978	*Back To The Egg* Wings
6th December 1978	*Wings Greatest* Wings

54 Twenty Beatle Fanzines

Fanzines are good fun. Produced by fans, aimed at fans, they are informative, personal and a good read. Here are twenty current fanzines of interest to Beatlefans.

1 *Beatlefan* Bill King, The Goody Press, Box 33515, Decatur, Georgia, GA 30033, USA. Expertly produced, crammed with information.

2 *Beatles Unlimited* P.O. Box 602, 340ap, Nieuwegeln, Netherlands. Highly recommended Dutch fanzine, printed in English.

3 *Beatles Beat* Royce Hurt, 702 South Main Street, Ripley, Mississippi, MS 38663, USA. There are special issues reproducing selections of clippings.

4 *Beatles Video Newsletter* John Dobrydnio, 184 Emerson Street, Springfield, Massachusetts, MA 01118, USA. Specialises in Beatles' films and videos.

5 *Beatles Now* Roger Akehurst, 73 Kitchener Road, Walthamstow, London E17, UK. Professionally printed bi-monthly, the best of the British 'zines.

6 *Cavern Mecca* Matthew Street, Liverpool, Merseyside L2 6RE, UK. Essential to any Beatlefan, Liverpool's own fanzine, with lots of local atmosphere.

7 *Club Sandwich* Wings Fun Club, P.O. Box 4UP, London W1A 4UP, UK. Official magazine of the Fun Club, professionally produced, everything you want to know about Paul and Linda.

8 *Good Day Sunshine* Charles F. Rosenay, 297 Edgewood Avenue, New Haven, Connecticut, CT 06511, USA. Lots of news, photographs and informative articles.

9 *Instant Karma* Marsha Ewing, P.O. Box 256, Sault Sainte Marie, Michigan, MI 49783, USA. The ultimate fanzine for John and Yoko folk.

The new glossy British Fanzine *Beatles Now*, has ambitious plans for expansion.

Instant Karma: the most detailed and regular source of John and Yoko stories.

10 *From Me To You* Peter Schuster. Postfach 555, 6430 Bad Hersfeld, West Germany. German language fanzine with English language supplement.

11 *The Harrison Alliance* Patti Murawski. 67 Cypress Street, Bristol, Connecticut, CT 06010, USA. Specialises in news on George.

12 *The McCartney Observer* Doylene Kindsvater, 220E 12th St., LaCrosse Kansas, KS 67548, USA. The 'zine for the Paul and Linda fans.

13 *Revolver* Gwyn Jenkins, 37 Hare Hill Close, Pyrford, Woking, Surrey GU22 8UH, UK. Modest, but enthusiastic publication.

14 *With A Little Help From My Friends* Pat Simmons, 10290 Pleasant Lake, No. F21, Cleveland, Ohio, OH 44130, USA. One of the premier American 'zines, with something for everyone.

15 *The Write Thing* Barb Whatmough. 3310 Roosevelt Ct., Minneapolis, Minnesota, MN 55418, USA. Of particular interest to collectors, by one of fandom's leading experts.

16 *Tomorrow Never Knows* Andy Hayles, 86 Shebury Road, Thorpe Bay, Essex, UK. Modest but enthusiastic publication.

17 *The Fab Four* Jacques Volcouve, Club des 4 de Liverpool, 43 bis, Boulevard Henri IV – 75004 Paris, France. Superbly produced magazine in the French language.

18 *Ram On* David Dunn, 8 Johnson Drive, Cambuslang, Glasgow, Scotland. Modest but worthwhile fanzine from the Paul McCartney fan club of Scotland.

19 *Yesterday* Beatles Fan Club Osterreich, c/o Andreas Roschal, Castlegasse, 1/30, 1210 Wien, Austria. A product of the Austrian fan club.

20 *Beatles Nytt* The Beatles Information Centre, Box 7481, S-103 92, Stockholm, Sweden. Pleasant fanzine from the Swedish club, similar in visual appeal to *Beatles Unlimited*.

55 Woolerisms

One of the most important figures on the Mersey Beat scene was Bob Wooler, originally a compere at various local halls before becoming resident d.j. at the Cavern Club. *Mersey Beat* readers would delight at his colourful, alliterative style of writing in columns where he would describe the Beatles as 'rhythmic revolutionaries' and shady agents as 'those characters from consville'. Bob would also compose advertisements for local promoters for both the *Liverpool Echo* and *Mersey Beat*. He was to coin many names which were known as 'Woolerisms' in deference to 'Goldwynisms'. They included:

The Nemperor: Brian Epstein
The Best of Cellars: The Cavern
Mr. Showmanship: Rory Storm
The Boswell Of Beat: Bill Harry
The Sheik Of Shake: Karl Terry (leader of the Cruisers)
The Panda Footed Prince Of Prance: Faron (leader of Faron's Flamingos)
Sock 'N' Sole Eleven: Suggestion for a rock soccer team which became the Mersey Beat XI

56 Historic Five

On 31st March 1964, the Beatles made recording history by securing the first five places in the American Top Hundred singles chart. The placings were:

No. 1 *Twist & Shout*
No. 2 *Can't Buy Me Love*
No. 3 *She Loves You*
No. 4 *I Want To Hold Your Hand*
No. 5 *Please Please Me*

57 Toppermost Of The Poppermost

Eight Beatles' singles immediately leapt to the No. 1 position in the UK during the first week of release. They were:

I Want To Hold Your Hand
Can't Buy Me Love
A Hard Day's Night
I Feel Fine
Ticket To Ride
Help!
Day Tripper/We Can Work It Out
Get Back

58 Title Tattle

Of the 200 books written about the fab Four, the most frequently used title has been the most obvious. There have been nine books which have simply been entitled *The Beatles*, and there will no doubt be many more:

1 *The Beatles* (1964) Norman Parkinson
2 *The Beatles* (1968) Anthony Scaduto
3 *The Beatles* (1974) Patrician Pirmangton
4 *The Beatles* (1975) Dezo Hoffman
5 *The Beatles* (1980) Geoffrey Stokes
6 *The Beatles* (1981) Alan Clark
7 *The Beatles* (1983) Robert Burt/Jeremy Pascall
8 *The Beatles* (1983) Helen Spence
9 *The Beatles* (1971) Aram Saroyan

Other Beatles' book titles which have been duplicated include:

Help! (1965) Author uncredited
Help! (1965) Al Hine

The John Lennon Story (1975) George Tremlett
The John Lennon Story (1981) John Swenson
Paul McCartney & Wings (1977) Jeremy Pascall
Paul McCartney & Wings (1977) Tony Jasper
A Hard Day's Night (1964) John Burke
A Hard Day's Night (1977) Philip DiFranco
The Beatles Forever (1978) Nicholas Schaffner
The Beatles Forever (1982) Helen Spence. Reprinted the following year as *The Beatles*
John Lennon. 1940–1980 (1981) Ernest E. Schworck
John Lennon. 1940–1980 (1981) Ray Connolly

The most ridiculous title of a Beatle book was probably *Communism, Hypnotism And The Beatles* by the Rev. A. Noebel, who also penned *The Beatles: A Study In Sex, Drugs & Revolution* and *John Lennon: Charming Or Harming A Generation*.

59 Preston Guesting

Billy Preston was a musician who the Beatles met as early as 1962 but it was not until 1969 that he became the first musician, apart from the Beatles themselves, to be credited on a Beatles' single.

George Harrison later produced his records for release on the Apple label and he appeared on several solo albums by individual members of the Fab Four. His appearances on Beatles' recordings are:

Let It Be
I, Me, Mine
I've Got A Feelin
Dig A Pony
One After 909
Get Back

His appearances on solo projects for John, George and Ringo included contributions to the following albums:

All Things Must Pass
The Concert For Bangla Desh
Extra Texture
Dark Horse
Thirty Three and A Third
Sometime In New York City
Ringo
Goodnight Vienna

60 Come Together

John and Paul became one of the most successful songwriting
partnerships of all time. They wrote a great number of songs
together, particularly in the early days, but eventually began to
write as individuals, whilst still crediting each song as a Lennon
& McCartney composition. On a number of songs, either John
or Paul made the main contribution with either a few suggestions, some lines or a middle eight coming from the other.
Here is a breakdown of the main Lennon & McCartney numbers, indicating who actually wrote them:

Lennon & McCartney
A Day In The Life
All You Need Is Love
Any Time At All
Baby's In Black
Baby, You're A Rich Man
Birthday
Can't Buy Me Love (mainly Paul)
Drive My Car
Eight Days A Week
Eleanor Rigby (mainly Paul)
Every Little Thing
From Me To You
Hold Me Tight (mainly Paul)
I Wanna Be Your Man (mainly Paul)
I Want To Hold Your Hand
I'll Get You

I've Got a Feeling
Little Child
Michelle (mainly Paul)
She Loves You
She's Leaving Home (mainly Paul)
Thank You Girl
The Word
Wait
What You Are Doing
Yellow Submarine

Paul McCartney
All My Loving
All Together Now
And I Love Her
Another Girl
Back In The USSR
The End
Fixing A Hole
The Fool On The Hill
For No One
Getting Better
Golden Slumbers/Carry That Weight
Good Day Sunshine
Got To Get You Into My Life
Hello Goodbye
Her Majesty
Blackbird
Get Back
Helter Skelter
Here, There And Everywhere
Hey Jude
Honey Pie
I Saw Her Standing There
I Will
I'll Follow The Sun
I'll Keep You Satisfied
I'm Down
I'm Looking Through You

I've Just Seen A Face
Lady Madonna
Let It Be
The Long & Winding Road
Love Me Do
Lovely Rita
Maxwell's Silver Hammer
Magical Mystery Tour
Mother Nature's Son
The Night Before
Oh, Darling
One And One Is Two
Penny Lane
P.S. I Love You
Paperback Writer
Rocky Raccoon
Ob-La-Di-Ob-La-Da
She Came In Through The Bathroom Window
She's A Woman
Tell Me What You See
Things We Said Today
Two Of Us
We Can Work It Out
When I'm Sixty Four
Wild Honey Pie
Why Don't We Do It In The Road
With A Little Help From My Friends
World Without Love
Yesterday
You Never Give Me Your Money
You Won't See Me
You Mother Should Know

John Lennon
A Hard Day's Night
Across The Universe
All I've Got To Do
And Your Bird Can Sing
Bad To Me

Because
Being For The Benefit Of Mr. Kite
Come Together
Cry Baby Cry
Day Tripper
Dear Prudence
Dig A Pony
Do You Want To Know A Secret
Don't Let Me Down
Dr. Robert
The Continuing Story Of Bungalow Bill
Everybody's Got Something To Hide. . .
Ballad Of John & Yoko
Girl
Glass Onion
Good Morning, Good Morning
Goodnight
Happiness Is A Warm Gun
Hey Bulldog
I Am The Walrus
I Call Your Name
I Feel Fine
I Don't Want To Spoil The Party
I Should Have Known Better
I Want You (She's So Heavy)
I'll Be Back
I'm Only Sleeping
I'm So Tired
In My Life
It Won't Be Long
It's Only Love
Julia
Lucy In The Sky With Diamonds
Mean Mr. Mustard
Misery
No Reply
Norwegian Wood
Not A Second Time
Nowhere Man

One After 909
Please Please Me
Polythene Pam
Rain
Revolution
Run For Your Life
She Said, She Said
Sexy Sadie
Sun King
This Boy
Tomorrow Never Knows
Yer Blues
You Can't Do That
You Know My Name (Look Up The Number)
What Goes On?

61 The Ivor Novello Awards

Annual awards presented by the Songwriter's Guild of Great Britain and named in honour of the late, famous British composer Ivor Novello. The Beatles' awards were:

OCTOBER 1964
1 The most outstanding contribution to British music in 1963
2 The most broadcast song   *She Loves You*
3 The top-selling record   *She Loves You*
4 Second top-selling record   *I Want To Hold Your Hand*
5 Second most outstanding song of the year   *All My Loving*

JULY 1966
1 The top-selling single of 1965   *We Can Work It Out*
2 The most outstanding song of the year   *Yesterday*
3 The second top-selling single of 1965   *Help!*

MARCH 1967
1 The most performed work of 1966   *Michelle*
2 The best-selling single of 1966   *Yellow Submarine*

119

62 Frost Go The Beatles

David Frost has been a major British TV celebrity and chat show host since the early sixties and also made the transition to American TV in the seventies. He had the individual members of the group appear on several of his shows. They include:

The David Frost Show (30th September 1967) John and George made an appearance on the show discussing meditation. It was so well received they were asked back for a further discussion.

The Frost Programme (27th December 1967) Paul made an appearance, discussing *Magical Mystery Tour*.

Frost On Sunday (8th September 1968) The Beatles made an appearance performing *Hey Jude* and *Revolution*.

The David Frost Show (23rd February 1969) Paul made an appearance to introduce Mary Hopkin.

The David Frost Show (29th March 1970) Ringo made an appearance and sang *Sentimental Journey*.

The David Frost Show (3rd December 1971) George made an appearance on the American version of the show.

The David Frost Show (13th January 1972) John and Yoko made an appearance on the show, which was televised from New York.

David Frost also hosted the American show: *Beatles Special* 21st May 1975 and a similar show in 1977.

63 *Mersey Beat*: The Contributors

For a tiny music paper, tucked away in a forgotten corner of the UK in 1961, the publication was to find several contributors who, in later years, were to find success in other fields. Here are just ten of them:

1   **John Lennon** His story of the Beatles' origins was the first published article on the band and his *Beatcomber* columns were to form the basis of his later books.

On the Cavern stage – two of Mersey Beat's contributors. The one on the right is Beatcomber!

2 **Paul McCartney** His letters to me were used as a series of small articles.

3 **Brian Epstein** He contributed record reviews and became deeply enmeshed in the local scene.

4 **Cilla Black** She once wrote a fashion column. Her name was Priscilla White, but as she hadn't signed her copy I made a mistake and credited it to Cilla Black.

5 **Mike McCartney** He contributed photographs using the name Francis Michael. He was later to become famous using the pseudonym Mike McGear.

6 **Bernard Falk** Journalist who penned 'The Moving Finger' column. He is a major British television interviewer.

7 **Roy Carr** Young musician from Blackpool who went on to become Special Projects Editor of the *New Musical Express* and co-author of *The Beatles Illustrated Record*

8 **Alan Smith** Our London correspondent who later became the editor of the *New Musical Express*. His wife Mavis was to join the Apple press office.

9 **Bob Azurdia** Columnist who became one of the major disc jockeys on Radio Merseyside.

10 **Brian Cooke** local artist who contributed hilarious adventures of a group called 'The Cuspidors'. He was to become one of Britain's leading cartoonists.

64 The Name's The Same

Several books have been written adopting the name of a Beatle's song as their actual title. They include:

Love Me Do Published by Penguin Books in paperback form in 1964. penned by Michael Braun, a New York writer who travelled to Cambridge, York, London, Liverpool, Paris, Washington and New York with the band. It is an observer's eye view of their touring days, subtitled: *The Beatles' Progress.*

British releases continued to be issued in a sequence exactly 20 years following the original release – with the result that the Beatles will continue to appear in the charts for many years to come.

Paperback Writer Published in 1978 by Grosset and Dunlap in the USA and New English Library in the UK. A comedy novel, penned by American rock writer Mark Shipper, it is a parody of the group's career, illustrated with spoof photographs.

All Together Now Published by Pierian Press in the USA in 1976, a complete discography of Beatles' products from 1961 to 1975 assembled with loving care by Harry Castleman and Walter J. Podrazik.

A Day In The Life Published by Pierian Press in the USA in 1980, a day-by-day account of the Beatles' activities between the years 1960 and 1970, compiled by Tom Schultheiss.

Things We Said Today Published by Pierian Press in the USA in 1980, the complete lyrics and a concordance to the Beatles' songs between the years 1962 and 1970, compiled by Colin Campbell and Allan Murphy.

You Can't Do That Published by Pierian Press in the USA in 1981, a discography of Beatles' bootlegs and novelty records from 1963–1980, compiled by Charles Reinhart.

The Long And Winding Road Published by Virgin Books in the UK in 1981, a history of the Beatles' records, detailing background stories of their songs, penned by Neville Stannard.

Here, There & Everywhere Published by Pierian Press in the USA in 1984, a bibliography.

65 The Beatles' London Clubs

The Ad Lib Leicester Street, Fashionable club for celebrities. John and Cynthia and George and Pattie visited the club on the night of their first LSD trip, and while in the lift, thought the club was on fire. It turned out they were freaked by the electric light bulb!

The Bag O'Nails Kingley Street. Club run by the Gunnell's, two brothers associated with London R & B acts, most of whom frequented the club, which was a haunt for Alan Price, Chris Farlowe and Georgie Fame. In fact, Georgie Fame was on stage the night Linda Eastman first met Paul McCartney here.

The Revolution Club Bruton Street. Record executives, particularly those from Polydor, rubbed shoulders with Paul McCartney, Led Zeppelin, Julie Driscoll and ex-rolling Stone Brian Jones, whilst being entertained by such acts as Yes, The Edwin Hawkins Singers, Terry Reid and Ike & Tina Turner.

The Scotch Of St. James Mason's Yard. Compact, warm club with tartan on the walls whose other regulars included the Rolling Stones and the Animals.

The Speakeasy Margaret Street. The Beatles were present at celebrity parties during the Apple days, enjoying the fun with artists ranging from Lulu to the Monkees. It was a favourite haunt of road managers.

Sibilla's Swallow Street. Named after Sybil Burton, ex-wife of actor Richard Burton, this trendy venue, tucked away in a small street off Regent Street, counted George Harrison as one of its backers. Paul McCartney often dropped into the club, sometimes in the company of Jane Asher.

Tramps Jermyn Street. Ringo escorted his glamorous girl friends to this luxurious celebrity spot, used as the inspiration for Jackie Collins' script of *The Bitch*. Marianne Faithfull, Mickie Most and Chinn & Chapman were among the regulars.

All of the clubs, with the exception of Tramps, eventually closed, although some of them re-opened under different names (The Revolution as Burlesque, The Speakeasy as Bootleggers, etc).

66 *Thank Your Lucky Stars*

A now defunct British pop music show, produced in Birmingham by ABC TV in the sixties. The Beatles made their first national television appearance on the show in January, 1963. Their performances on the programme included:

1963: 11th January; 29th June; 26th October; 22nd December
1964: 11th July; 11th November
1965: 3rd April; 17th July; 4th December
1966: 18th June

67 Brit Hits

A number of the songs penned by Lennon & McCartney and John, Paul and George individually, have reached the British Top 50 when recorded by other artists. Here is a list of those successes, excluding the several discs such as the Trends' *All My Loving* and the Rezillos' *I Wanna Be Your Man*, which had chart placings, but never actually reached the Top 50 itself. I am also excluding the several records which were hits in the USA only.

1 *All My Loving* Recorded by the Dowlands, it reached No. 33 in January 1964.

2 *A Hard Day's Night* Recorded by Peter Sellers, it reached No. 14 in December 1965.

3 *A World Without Love* Recorded by Peter & Gordon, it reached No. 1 in April 1964.

4 *Bad To Me* Recorded by Billy J. Kramer & The Dakotas, it reached No. 1 in August 1963.

5 *Come & Get It* Recorded by Badfinger, it reached No. 4 in January 1970.

6 *Day Tripper* Recorded by Otis Redding. It reached No. 43 in March 1977.

7 *Dear Prudence* Recorded by Siouxsie, it reached No. 2 in 1983.

8 *Do You Want To Know A Secret?* Recorded by Billy J. Kramer & The Dakotas. It reached No. 2 in May 1963.

9 *Can't Buy Me Love* Recorded by Ella Fitzgerald. It reached No. 30 in May 1964.

10 *Eleanor Rigby* Recorded by Ray Charles. It reached No. 36 in July 1968. In the USA, it reached No. 35

11 *Girl* Recorded by the St. Louis Union. It reached No. 25 in January 1966.

12 *Girl* Recorded by Truth. It reached No. 19 in February 1966.

13 *Golden Slumbers/Carry That Weight* Recorded by Trash. It reached No. 35 in October 1969.

14 *Got To Get You Into My Life* Recorded by Cliff Bennett & The Rebel Rousers. It reached No. 8 in August 1966.

15   *Got To Get You Into My Life* Recorded by Earth, Wind & Fire. It reached No. 30 in October 1978. In the USA, it reached No. 4.

16   *Goodbye* Recorded by Mary Hopkin. It reached No. 2 in April 1969.

17   *Govinda* Recorded by the Radha Krishna Temple. It reached No. 12 in March 1970.

18   *Help!* Recorded by Tina Turner. It reached No. 40 in March 1984.

19   *Here, There & Everywhere* Recorded by Emmylou Harris. It reached No. 28 in March, 1976.

20   *Hey Jude* Recorded by Wilson Pickett. It reached No. 29 in January 1969.

21   *Here Comes The Sun* Recorded by Steve Harley & Cockney Rebel. It reached No. 27 in July 1976.

22   *Get Back* Recorded by Rod Stewart. It reached No. 10 in November 1976.

23   *Hello Little Girl* Recorded by the Fourmost. It reached No. 10 in September 1963.

24   *From A Window* Recorded by Billy J. Kramer & the Dakotas. It reached No. 10 in July 1964.

25   *I'll Keep You Satisfied* Recorded by Billy J. Kramer & The Dakotas. It reached No. 4 in November 1963.

26   *I'm In Love* Recorded by the Fourmost. It reached No. 12 in January 1964.

27   *It's For You* Recorded by Cilla Black. It reached No. 8 in August 1964.

28   *I Wanna Hold Your Hand* Recorded by Dollar. It reached No. 9 in November 1979.

29   *It's Only Love* Recorded by Bryan Ferry and issued as part of an EP record. It reached No. 7 in August 1976.

30   *I Should Have Known Better* Recorded by the Naturals. It reached No. 9 in August 1964.

31   *I Wanna Be Your Man* Recorded by the Rolling Stones. It reached No. 9 in January 1964.

32   *I Saw Her Standing There* Recorded by Elton John and issued as part of an EP record. It reached No. 24 in April 1981.

33   *If I Needed Someone* Recorded by the Hollies. It reached the position of No. 24 in December 1965.

34 *Lucy In The Sky With Diamonds* Recorded by Elton John. It reached No. 8 in November 1974.

35 *Love Of The Loved* Recorded by Cilla Black. It reached No. 30 in October 1963.

36 *Like Dreamers Do* Recorded by the Applejacks. It reached No. 23 in June 1964.

37 *The Long & Winding Road* Recorded by Ray Morgan. It reached No. 32 in July 1970.

38 *Michelle* Recorded by the Overlanders. It reached No. 1 in January 1966.

39 *Michelle* Recorded by David & Jonathan. It reached No. 11 in June 1964.

40 *Nobody I Know* Recorded by Peter & Gordon. It reached No. 9 in June 1964.

41 *Nowhere Man* Recorded by Three Good Reasons. It reached No. 47 in March 1966.

42 *Ob-La-Di-Ob-La-Da* Recorded by the Bedrocks. It reached No. 17 in December 1968.

43 *Ob-La-Di-Ob-La-Da* Recorded by the Marmalade. It reached No. 1 in December 1968.

44 *Fool On The Hill* Recorded by Shirley Bassey. It reached No. 48 in January 1971.

45 *Please Please Me* Recorded by David Cassidy. It reached No. 16 in July 1974.

46 *Step Inside Love* Recorded by Cilla Black. It reached No. 7 in March 1968.

47 *Something* Recorded by Shirley Bassey. It reached No. 4 in June 1970.

48 *That Means A Lot* Recorded by P. J. Proby. It reached No. 24 in November 1965.

49 *Woman* Recorded by Peter & Gordon. It reached No. 22 in February 1966.

50 *With A Little Help From My Friends* Recorded by Joe Brown, it reached No. 32 in June 1967.

51 *With A Little Help From My Friends* Recorded by Joe Cocker. It reached No. 1 in November 1968.

52 *With A Little Help From My Friends* Recorded by Young Idea. It reached No. 29 in July 1967.

53 *When I'm Sixty Four* Recorded by Kenny Ball & His

Jazzmen. It reached No. 43 in July 1967.

54 *We Can Work It Out* Recorded by Stevie Wonder. It reached No. 22 in May 1971. In the USA it reached the position of No. 9.

55 *Yesterday* Recorded by Matt Monro. It reached No. 36 in November 1965.

56 *Yesterday* Recorded by Ray Charles. It reached No. 44 in December 1967. In the USA it reached the position of No. 25.

57 *You've Got To Hide Your Love Away* Recorded by the Silkie. It reached No. 29 in September 1965.

68 'Insider' Books

Of the approximately 200 books which have been published concerning the Beatles, a handful have been written by people who were friends, associates, relatives or had first-hand experience of their life and career. A number of books, of course, remain unpublished. It is interesting to note that John's father Alfred penned an autobiography; Mal Evans, the Beatles friend, road manager and personal assistant, also completed a book before he died. The manuscript appears to be lost and some say its title was *Living the Beatles Legend*. Pat Delaney, doorman of the Cavern club, wrote a book of his experiences called *The Best Of Cellars*.

The 'insider' books continue to be published as various associates declare their intention to put pen to paper. Books we can expect in the future include Jimmy Nicol's memories of his 1964 world tour as replacement for the sick Ringo; Dick Rowe's confessions as *The Man Who Turned Down The Beatles*; Gerry Bernstein's book about her husband, *The Man Who Brought The Beatles To America*. Terry Doran, their friend and the former manager of Apple Music is currently at work on a book and Yoko Ono was offered a reputed 5 million dollars for her *A Widow's Tale*. The 'insider' books include:

A Cellarful Of Noise (1964) By Brian Epstein. Souvenir Press, UK/Doubleday, USA. The book also became available in paperback from Pyramid in the USA and New English Library in the UK. Their former manager's biography was ghosted by his aide Derek Taylor and is a personal view of the period from the time Brian signed the Beatles to their rise to fame in the UK 2 years later.

Murray The K Tells It Like It Is, Baby (1966) By Murray Kaufman, published in the USA by Holt, Rinehart & Winston. The New York disc jockey who was a self-proclaimed 'fifth Beatle' tells of his association with the band.

The Longest Cocktail Party (1972) By Richard DiLello. Published by Playboy Press in the USA and Charisma Books in the UK. An hilarious diary of events covering the bizarre world of the Apple organisation by one of its press officers.

Body Count (1972) By Francie Schwartz. Published in the USA by Straight Arrow Books. Francie, an American girl who lived with Paul McCartney for a short time, recalls this love affair and several others.

As Time Goes By (1973) By Derek Taylor. Published in the USA by Straight Arrow Books and in the UK by Abacus Books. Written in an unusual style, to say the least. Memories of the sixties as Derek relates fragments of his life with the Beatles and other bands.

The Man Who Gave The Beatles Away (1975) by Alan Williams and William Marshall. There have been several editions of this book, including the American Ballantine Books' edition and the Elm Tree Books' British edition. A Liverpool clubowner who booked the Beatles for their first Hamburg trip has his reminiscences put to paper by journalist William Marshall.

Linda's Pictures (1976) Linda McCartney's album of photographs. She has continued issuing photo-books, including one simply entitled *Photographs*, issued by Pavilion Books in the UK in 1982.

Mersey Beat: The Beginnings of The Beatles (1977) By Bill Harry. Published by Omnibus Press. A selection of Beatles' material from the pages of the legendary paper.

John Lennon: One Day At A Time By Anthony Fawcett. Published by Grove Press in the USA and New English Library in the UK. John and Yoko's former personal assistant relates his adventures during his years with the duo.

A Twist Of Lennon (1978) Originally published in the UK as a paperback by Star Books. Cynthia Lennon, John's first wife, takes a trip down memory lane.

Rock 'n' Roll Times (1981) By Jurgen Vollmer. Google Plex Books in the USA followed in the footsteps of a Paris publishing firm in issuing this slim volume of photographs. Jurgen was a German photographer who became a friend of the Beatles during the first trip to Hamburg.

All You Need Is Ears (1979) By George Martin. Published in the UK by Macmillan, this hardback book has the Beatles' recording manager recounting his experiences, which are presented in a breezy style by freelance journalist Jeremy Hornsby.

Thank U Very Much (1981) By Mike McCartney. Published in the UK by Arthur Baker, this handsome production has Paul's younger brother revealing the family history, with lots of photographs and memorabilia.

The Love You Make (1983) By Peter Brown. Published in the USA by McGraw-Hill and in Britain by Macmillan, Brian Epstein's former personal assistant has produced a 'kiss and tell' book, ghosted for him by rock journalist, Steven Gaines.

With The Beatles (1982) By Dezo Hoffman, published in the UK by Omnibus Press. A Hungarian photographer, based in London in the early sixties, records various events at the time of the group's initial record success, in a collection of photographs with his personal comments. He has had several of his Beatles' photo-books published previously in Japan and the USA.

Loving John (1983) By May Pang. Published in the USA by Grosset & Dunlap and in Britain by Corgi Books. John's former mistress reveals details of her love affair in a 'kiss and tell' book, co-written with Henry Edwards.

Beatle (1984) By Pete Best. Plexus Books in the UK finally publish the memoirs of Pete, who was drummer with the Beatles in the 2 years prior to them releasing their first British single. Show business writer Pat Doncaster has encouraged him to talk – over 20 years after he originally left the group.

Fifty Years Adrift (In An Open-Necked Shirt) (Not yet published) By Derek Taylor. Published in a limited edition of 2,000 signed copies by Genesis Books, who produced *I; Me; Mine,* this is the second book of Taylor's recollections.

69 From *Please Please Me* to *Let It Be*

Track-listings of Beatles' original British album releases.

Please Please Me
I Saw Her Standing There; Misery; Anna (Go To Him); Chains; Boys; Ask Me Why; Please Please Me; Love Me Do; P.S. I Love You; Baby It's You; Do You Want To Know A Secret?; A Taste Of Honey; There's A Place; Twist & Shout.

With The Beatles
It Won't Be Long; All I've Got To Do; All My Loving; Don't Bother Me; Little Child; Till There Was You; Please Mr. Postman; Roll Over Beethoven; Hold Me Tight; You Really Got A Hold On Me; I Wanna Be Your Man; Devil In Her Heart; Not A Second Time; Money (That's What I Want).

A Hard Day's Night
A Hard Day's Night; I Should Have Known Better; If I Fell; I'm Happy Just To Dance With You; And I Love Her; Tell Me Why; Can't Buy Me Love; Any Time At All; I'll Cry Instead; Things We Said Today; When I Get Home; You Can't Do That; I'll Be Back.

Beatles For Sale
No Reply; I'm A Loser; Baby's In Black; Rock and Roll Music; I'll Follow The Sun; Mr. Moonlight; Kansas City/Hey Hey Hey; Eight Days A Week; Words Of Love; Honey Don't; Every Little Thing; I Don't Want To Spoil The Party; What You're Doing; Everybody's Trying To Be My Baby.

Help!
Help!; The Night Before; You've Got To Hide Your Love Away; I Need You; Another Girl; You're Going To Lose That Girl; Ticket To Ride; Act Naturally; It's Only Love; You Like Me Too Much; Tell Me What You See; I've Just Seen A Face; Yesterday; Dizzy Miss Lizzy.

Rubber Soul
Drive My Car; Nowegian Wood (This Bird Has Flown); You Won't See Me; Nowhere Man; Think For Yourself; The Word; Michelle; What Goes on; Girl; I'm Looking Through You; In My Life; Wait; If I Needed Someone; Run For Your Life.

Revolver

Taxman; Eleanor Rigby; I'm Only Sleeping; Love You Too; Here, There & Everywhere; Yellow Submarine; She Said, She Said; Good Day Sunshine; And Your Bird Can Sing; For No One; Dr. Robert; I Want To Tell You; Got To Get You Into My Life; Tomorrow Never Knows.

Sgt. Pepper's Lonely Hearts Club Band

Sgt. Pepper's Lonely Hearts Club Band; With A Little Help From My Friends; Lucy In The Sky With Diamonds; Getting Better; Fixing A Hole; She's Leaving Home; Being For The Benefit Of Mr. Kite; Within You, Without You; When I'm Sixty-Four; Lovely Rita; Good Morning, Good Morning; Sgt. Pepper's Lonely Hearts Club Band; A Day In The Life.

The Beatles

Back In The USSR; Dear Prudence; Glass Onion; Ob-La-Di-Ob-La-Da; Wild Honey Pie; The Continuing Story Of Bungalow Bill; While My Guitar Gently Weeps; Happiness Is A Warm Gun; Martha My Dear; I'm So Tired; Blackbird; Piggies; Rocky Raccoon; Don't Pass Me By; Why Don't We Do It In The Road; I Will; Julia; Yer Blues; Mother Nature's Son; Everybody's Got Something To Hide Except Me And My Monkey; Sexy Sadie; Helter Skelter; Long, Long, Long; Revolution; Honey Pie; Savoy Truffle; Cry Baby Cry; Revolution 9; Goodnight.

Yellow Submarine

Yellow Submarine; Only A Northern Song; All Together Now; Hey Bulldog; It's All Too Much; All You Need Is Love.

Abbey Road

Come Together; Something; Maxwell's Silver Hammer; Oh Darling; Octopus's Garden; I Want You (She's So Heavy); Here Comes The Sun; Because; You Never Give Me Your Money; Sun King; Mean Mr. Mustard; Polythene Pam; She Came In Through The Bathroom Window; Golden Slumbers; Carry That Weight; The End; Her Majesty.

Let It Be

Two Of Us; Dig A Pony; Across The Universe; I. Me. Mine; Dig It; Let It Be; Maggie May; I've Got A Feeling; One After 909; The Long and Winding Road; For You Blue; Get Back.

70 The Hamburg Tracks

During December, 1962, Adrian Barber, former member of Liverpool band the Big Three, recorded the Beatles live on stage at the Star Club in Hamburg, when he was the stage manager there. Adrian was testing the acoustics, as he was building a complete new sound system for the club, which was also to include a recording system. Ted Taylor, leader of another Liverpool band, Kingsize Taylor & The Dominoes, asked Adrian if he could have the tapes. They were forgotten about for many years until a Liverpool promotion in the mid-seventies in which Kingsize Taylor was appearing. He chatted to Alan Williams and mentioned the tapes. They eventually emerged on a double album *The Beatles Live! At The Star Club In Hamburg, Germany, 1962* and have been re-issued under various titles ever since. The full track listing is as follows:

I Saw Her Standing There
Roll Over Beethoven
Hippy Hippy Shake
Sweet Little Sixteen
Lend Me Your Comb
Your Feet's Too Big
Twist & Shout
Mr. Moonlight
A Taste Of Honey
Besame Mucho
Reminiscing
Kansas City/Hey Hey Hey
Nothin' Shakin' (But The Leaves On The Trees)
To Know Her Is To Love Her
Little Queenie
Falling In Love Again
Ask Me Why
Be-Bop-A-Lula
Hallelujah, I Love Her So
Red Sails In The Sunset
Everybody's Trying To Be My Baby

Matchbox
I'm Talking About You
Shimmy Shimmy
Long Tall Sally
I Remember You
Twist & Shout
Falling In Love Again

71 The Fifth Beatle

Over the years, a handful of people have been referred to as
'The Fifth Beatle.' To be honest, Brian Epstein is the only
person who actually deserves the name. Here are six of the
contenders:

Brian Epstein Their manager. Often called 'The Fifth Beatle'
because of his efforts in steering them to the top. They never
seemed to recover from his death as their direction vanished
when they lost him, despite the fact that he had less and less
actually to do on their behalf once they had been established as
the world's top show business attraction.

Stuart Sutcliffe Their former bass guitarist who was, for a
time, the actual fifth member of the group. He played with the
band in Liverpool and Hamburg and toured with them in Scotland. Stu then left the Beatles to pursue his artistic studies, but
died at the age of 21.

George Martin Their recording manager. Tagged 'The Fifth
Beatle' because of his contribution to their recorded sound. It
was a symbiotic relationship because Martin's technical exper-
tise and the Fab Four's musical innovations provided a revolution in popular music throughout the sixties.

Neil Aspinall The person who was with them longest. In at the
beginning, he outstayed all the rest, rising from the position of
humble road manager to administrator of their affairs in the
still-active Apple company.

Murray The K The late American disc jockey who died in
January 1982. As d.j. for the New York station WINS, he

134

STUART SUTCLIFFE (1940-62)

Paintings drawings & prints

Only in recent years have people begun to realise how genuinely talented Stuart Sutcliffe was as a painter.

latched on to the group when they arrived for their first American tour in February 1964, interviewing them at the Plaza Hotel, taking them to night clubs, following them to Florida – and even kipping down in George's hotel room. He was a self-styled 'Fifth Beatle' until Brian Epstein objected to him using the term.

Ed Rudy An American Journalist-announcer, who joined the Beatles on their American tour. He has since issued an album of his interviews entitled: *The Beatles American Tour With Ed Rudy* in which he announces: 'The Beatles call Ed Rudy "The Fifth Beatle" and after listening to these exclusive recordings YOU'LL KNOW WHY!!!'

72 The Hamburg Clubs

During their early career, the Beatles appeared at a number of clubs in the St. Pauli district of Hamburg, Germany. They were:

The Indra Their Hamburg club dubut took place at this relatively small club between August and October 1960. Typical of clubs in the area, it had a tough clientele and was run by a man called Bruno Koschmeider.

The Kaiser Keller The King's Cellar was another club owned by Koschmeider, situated further up the narrow Grosse Freiheit, but altogether a less seedier place than the Indra. The Indra was closed by the police early in October and Koschmeider moved the group across to his new club.

The Top Ten Club in the Reeperbahn, the main street of the St. Pauli area. The owner 'Peter Eckhorn' had booked Tony Sheridan and the Beatles agreed to appear there for one night in December 1960. A furious Bruno Koschmeider instigated action which led to the Beatles' return to Liverpool. The Fab Four set off for the Top Ten club again in April 1961 for a season lasting 3 months.

The Star Club The largest and most popular of the Hamburg clubs, opened by Manfred Weissleder on the site of a former cinema in the Grosse Freiheit. The Beatles were the stars of the club from the opening night on 13th April 1962 and their first season lasted until 31st May. Their second trip that year lasted from 1st November to 14th and their third and final Star Club appearance took place between 18th and 31st December, during which time Adrian Barber recorded their performances.

73 Lennon's Literary List

The initial books of interest to a Lennon fan are the two books which he wrote himself. There were only a handful of publications concerning John prior to his death, but an entire stream of books, mainly hurriedly written, were issued soon after he died. Since that time, there has been a steady stream of publications and, at the time of writing, there are a number of further Lennon books in the pipeline, including a further book by his first wife Cynthia, a Yoko Ono memoir tentatively titled *A Widow's Tale* and a hefty volume by Albert Goldman, author of the notorious best-seller Elvis.

In His Own Write (1964) Published by Jonathan Cape in the UK and Simon & Schuster in the USA. Also published in France under the title *In Flagrante Delire*. John Lennon's first collection of his stories and drawings, with an introduction by Paul and book design by Robert Freeman.

A Spaniard In the Works (1965) John's second book, issued by the same publishers as his previous offering.

The Penguin John Lennon (1966) Paperback book containing the complete material from John's two previous books.

The Lennon Play: In His Own Write (1968) By John Lennon, Adrienne Kennedy and Victor Spinetti. Published by Jonathan Cape in the UK and Simon & Schuster in the USA. American writer Adrienne Kennedy first had the idea of adapting John's book into a one-act play and Victor Spinetti helped her to write it. The play was produced twice and John and Yoko attended one of the premiers.

Lennon Remembers (1971) Originally published in the USA by Straight Arrow, the book arm of *Rolling Stone* magazine. The lengthy interviews which Jann Wenner conducted with John provide an interesting insight into John's own vision of the Beatles.

The Lennon Factor (1972) By Paul Young, published in the USA by Stein & Day. A slim volume of poetry with John as the main theme.

The John Lennon Story (1975) By George Tremlett, published as a paperback in the UK by Futura Books. The first detailed story of John's life , with a chronology included.

John Lennon: One Day At A Time (1976) By Anthony Fawcett, Published by Grove Press in the USA and New English Library in the UK. A fascinating account of John and Yoko's life and career during the period when Fawcett acted as their personal assistant. Lavishly illustrated.

John Lennon: Death Of A Dream (1980) By George Carpozi Jr. First book on the market following John's death. A paperback from Manor Books.

A Twist Of Lennon (1978) By Cynthia Lennon. Originally published in the UK by Star Books and in the USA in 1980 by Avon. John's first wife reminisces about their years together, adding poems and illstrations to her story.

Strawberry Fields Forever; John Lennon Remembered (1980) Another paperback rush-release, although better than most and containing a lengthy interview reprinted from *Newsweek* magazine.

John Lennon 1940–1980 (1980) French language book published by Artefact in Paris and compiled by Har van Fulpen.

Lennon: Up Close and Personal (1981) Written by Timothy Beckley and published in the USA by Sunshine Publications.

Lennon: What Happened! (1981) Written by Timothy Green and published in the USA by Sunshine Publications.

John Lennon & The Beatles Forever (1981) Another rush-release paperback, this time from Tower Books, edited by Ed Naha.

John Lennon 1940–1980 (1981) By Ray Connolly, published in the UK by Fontana Books. One of the literate and worthwhile Lennon books, written by someone who knew him personally.

John Lennon In His Own Words (1981) By Miles, published by Omnibus Press. One of a series of books containing rock star quotes. John's words of wit and wisdom over the years.

The Lennon Tapes (1981) BBC Publications. Complete transcript of the interviews conducted between John and disc Jockey Andy Peebles a short time before John's death.

John Lennon 1940–1980 (1981) Written by Ernest E. Schworck and published by ESE, California.

The John Lennon Story (1981) Written by John Swenson and published in the USA by Leisure Books.

A Tribute To John Lennon 1940–1980 (1981) Published by Proteus Books, a collection of tributes reprinted from various newspapers around the world.

The Playboy Interviews With John Lennon & Yoko Ono (1981) The complete text of interviews conducted by David Sheff, published in the USA by Playboy Press and in the UK by New English Library.

The Ballad Of John & Yoko (1982) Published by the Rolling Stone Press in the USA and by Michael Joseph in the UK. A selection of material on John from *Rolling Stone* magazine, compiled by the editors of *Rolling Stone.*

John Lennon's Secret (1983) By David Stuart Ryan, published by Kozmik Press in the UK. Well written biography with numerous photographs.

John Lennon: In My Life (1983) Published in the USA by Grove Press and in the UK by Coronet Books, written by Pete Shotton and Nicholas Schaffner. Pete was John's childhood friend and Nicholas compiled the book from 15 hours of interviews with him.

Loving John (1983) By May Pang and Henry Edwards, published in the USA by Warner Publishing and in the UK by Corgi. John and Yoko's former secretary and John's erstwhile lover, writes of the affair.

The John Lennon Family Album (1983) Lavish photo-book, published in a limited edition in Japan and available from a few specialist outlets. Photographer Nisni F. Salmaru presents over a hundred previously unpublished photographs of John, Yoko and Sean in Japan.

John Lennon: Summer Of 1980 (1983) Published by Perigee Books in the USA, a collection of pictures of John by eight different photographers, with an introduction by Yoko Ono.

Dakota Days (1983) By John Green. Published by St. Martin's Press in the USA, this is a 'kiss-and-tell' book by the Lennons' former tarot card reader. It's a sensationalised account of Green's days under John and Yoko's employ, which Yoko has condemned as being wildly inaccurate.

The Literary Lennon (1983) By James Sauceda. Another

Pierian Press production and an engrossing analysis of John's literary work, from his schooldays, through his *Mersey Beat* writings to his books and magazine articles.

Living With Lennon (1983) By Fred Seaman. Simon & Schuster announced publication of this book, although I haven't seen a copy yet. It is by John and Yoko's former assistant who had a dramatic end to his involvement with the Lennons.

John Winston Lennon (1940–1966) (1984) By Ray Coleman. Published in the UK by Sidgwick & Jackson, this is the first of Ray's 120,000-word books on the life of John, illustrated with some rare photographs, including previously unpublished pics by Astrid Kirchnerr.

John Ono Lennon (1967–1980) (1984) Hard on the heels of Ray's first book comes the final part in the epic story, the most diligently researched work on John yet published.

The Book Of Lennon (1984) Published in the UK by Aurum Press and in the USA by Delilah. An encyclopaedia containing hundreds of entries on John's books, records, films and songs.

Come Together: John Lennon In His Time (1985) By John Wiener. Published in the USA by Random House, an investigation of the FBI's part in the harrassment of John during his attempt to fight a deportation order.

74 Pepper Profiles

There were over sixty figures featured on the cover of the *Sgt.Pepper's Lonely Hearts Club Band* album. The Beatles' idea of posing in colourful costumes on a special set surrounded by people who tickled their fancy, was more or less a co-operative venture, with each member of the band contributing suggestions as to who should be included in the series of life-size cardboard cut-outs.

The montage was prepared by pop artist Peter Blake and his assistant was his wife Jan Haworth. The photograph was taken by Michael Cooper.

No one knows exactly how many names were originally suggested, although John Lennon put forward Hitler and Jesus, both of which were turned down by the others. The finished compendium is a strange blend of film stars, authors, psychiatrists, friends and fellow musicians. Of the sixty-two figures there are no less than five eastern holy men (or gurus), three unidentified girls and the four waxworks of the Beatles themselves (from Madame Tussaud's). The other members of the 'Sgt. Pepper Band' are:

Aldous Huxley British author, philosopher and mystic who died in 1963. His most famous novel is *Brave New World*, a contemporary classic. His non-fiction book *The Doors of Perception* explored the effects of hallucinogenic drugs on the senses, an exploration of the visions induced by mescalin and peyote. As the Beatles were becoming aware of the heightened consciousness produced by hallucinogenics, it is more than likely that John, at least, had read this book.

Diana Dors Buxom platinum blonde, one of Britain's major screen sex goddesses of the fifties and early sixties, the UK answer to Monroe/Mae West. In the seventies and early eighties, she put on a considerable amount of weight but her engaging personality ensured that she became a household name, appearing regularly on television, both as an actress and chat show host/guest. In 1981, she appeared on a video film promoting Adam Ant's single *Prince Charming* and became quite popular with the younger set.

Carl Gustav Jung Swiss-born psychiatrist who died in 1961. Throughout his life he was interested in mysteries: such as the occurrence of coincidences (which he referred to as 'synchronicity'), the content of dreams and whether ancient arts such as the I Ching could really prophesy accurately. Appropriately, before the Second World War he had a dream in which he saw the future. He was in Liverpool – and Liverpool was 'the city of light'. By a stretch of the imagination, one could say that he foresaw the birth of the Beatles!

Max Miller A tongue-in-the-cheek choice. The late Max Miller was a very popular British comedian known as 'the cheeky chappie' because of a comedy routine littered with double-entendres and near-the knuckle risqué jokes. Although successful on the music halls, Max was never able to make the transition to television because of the nature of his humour.

Lenny Bruce Cult American comedian who died through drug abuse. An abrasive club routine in which he insulted his audiences, using four-letter words liberally, caused much controversy and he was the subject of a film bio-pic in which he was portrayed by Dustin Hoffman.

Huntz Hall Fair-haired stooge of the Bowery Boys (The Bowery is an area in Lower Manhattan, New York) who were given their own series of second feature comedy films. In some ways, Hall bore a resemblance to Ringo Starr's friend Rory Storm.

Stuart Sutcliffe Former bass guitarist with the Beatles, who died in Hamburg of a brain haemmorhage in 1962 at the age of 21. John Lennon's close friend from the Liverpool College of Art, Stu was one of the most talented artists to emerge in Liverpool at the end of the fifties and it was because of a painting he sold at the John Moore's Exhibition at the Walker Art Gallery that he was able to afford his first guitar. His period as a member of the Beatles was brief and in 1983 interest was rekindled with a stage play *Stu*.

Dion American singer, born in 1939, who had his early hits fronting Dion & The Belmonts. He turned solo in 1960 and had a number of hits such as *Runaround Sue* and *The Wanderer*. His career took a downturn in 1964 around the time the Beatles conquered the USA, but he was to make several 'comebacks'.

Stephen Crane American author who wrote the enduring books *The Red Badge Of Courage* and *The Outcasts Of Poker Flat*. Like several of the other 'Pepper People', he was young, brilliant and suffered an early death, dying in 1900 from tuberculosis at the age of 28.

Fred Astaire The screen's most famous dancing star, noted for his inventive style of dancing and associated with top hat and tails, following films such as *Top Hat*, *Funny Face* and *Flying Down To Rio*. Born in 1899, Fred was one of the celebrities who John featured in his 1972 film *Imagine*.

William Burroughs American writer of experimental/drug/SF novels, born in 1914, who became very fashionable in the mid-sixties among British 'underground' groups, several of whom named themselves after the titles of his books. His first published work was entitled *Junkie* and others included *The Naked*

Lunch, The Soft Machine, The Ticket That Exploded and *Nova Express*. David Bowie was another musician inspired by his novels.

Aubrey Beardsley Like Stuart Sutcliffe, an intensely talented artist who died young. Beardsley suffered from ill health from the age of 6, but became one of the most famous and controversial of Victorian illustrators during a 6-year period when most of his innovative work was created. An associate of Oscar Wilde, Beardsley created a series of erotic drawings which almost ruined his career (John Lennon was also to create controversy with his erotic lithographs). He died at the age of 25.

Karheinz Stockhausen Contemporary German composer, born in 1928. He was a pioneer in the development of electronic sounds.

Johnny Weissmuller American actor/athlete, born in 1904, who became the US Swimming Champion and won five Gold Medals in the Olympic Games. He is most often remembered as the most popular screen Tarzan, appearing as the ape man in numerous films between the years 1932 and 1938.

H. G. Wells Novelist who, almost single-handedly, created many major science-fiction themes which are still popular today. Author of novels such as *The Invisible Man, The War Of The Worlds, The Time Machine* and *The Island Of Dr. Moreau*, all of which have been filmed, he died in 1946. His *The War Of The Worlds* was translated into a rock album by Jeff Wayne, with many British musicians appearing on it, and it became an international multi-million seller.

Mae West Famous screen sex symbol, born in Brooklyn, who starred in films such as *My Little Chickadee* and *Night After Night*. Her outrageous quotes titillated generations of cinema goers and a life-saving device was named after her. Beatles' publicist Derek Taylor once worked for her for a short spell and Ringo Starr was to appear in the film *Sextette* with her. She died in the early eighties.

Dr. David Livingstone Scots Missionary and explorer whose exploits on the Dark Continent in the nineteenth century captured the imagination of the Victorian age. Most schoolchildren remember the famous phrase when Stanley eventually found him: 'Dr Livingstone I presume?' He died in 1873.

George Bernard Shaw Irish-born British playwright who died in 1950. Shaw won the Nobel Prize for Literature in 1925 and among his considerable number of plays were *Caesar & Cleopatra*, *Man and Superman*, *Major Barbara*, *Pygmalion* and *St Joan*. Paul appeared as the Inquisitor in a Liverpool Institute production of *St. Joan*.

Dylan Thomas Welsh poet who died of an excess of alcohol in New York in 1953. He was also a playwright, penning works such as *Under Milk Wood*. He is said to have inspired a certain Mr. Zimmerman to use the name Bob Dylan.

Oscar Wilde Irish wit, author and playwright who died in ignominy in Paris in 1900. At one time famous and fêted among the aristocracy in London, he fell from favour when it was revealed that he was a homosexual and involved in a major scandal. His works include *The Picture Of Dorian Gray* and *The Importance of Being Earnest*.

Sonny Liston Boxer who became Heavyweight Boxing Champion of the World in 1962 when he knocked out Floyd Patterson. Tragically, he died a lonely death, his body only being found a week after he died in 1970. It was when he was due to fight Cassius Clay for the World Title that the Beatles visited Clay's training camp in 1964 – and the man who was later to become Mohammad Ali, enjoyed a great deal of publicity from the visit. He then went on to take the title from Liston. Could this inclusion be by way of an apology – or was it simply because artist Peter Blake owned the waxwork of the boxer which was used on the sleeve?

Stan Laurel One half of the famous comedy duo of Laurel & Hardy. Stan was born in the same county as the Beatles: Lancashire, and moved to the USA where he entered into partnership with Ollie in 1926. He died in 1965.

Oliver Hardy Together with his partner Stan Laurel, he created an enduring screen comedy partnership in such films as *Way Out West*. A song from that film, *Trail Of The Lonesome Pine*, provided the pair with a posthumous hit in the seventies. Ollie died in 1957.

Marilyn Monroe Tragic Hollywood sex goddess who died of an overdose of sleeping pills in 1962. She became famous in the fifties in such films as *How To Marry A Millionaire*, *The Seven*

Year Itch, Some Like It Hot and *The Misfits*. Her talent was under-rated during her lifetime but has been reassessed. Paul McCartney owns a sculpture of her.

W. C. Fields American comedian, born Clarke William Dukenfield in 1880. Famous for his quotable, cynical one-liners, his eccentric style of dress (including top hat and frayed gloves) and dead-pan humour, he made several major comedy films, including *My Little Chickadee* and *Never Give A Sucker An Even Break*. He died in 1946 and Rod Steiger portrayed him in a film bio-pic.

Tommy Handley Late Liverpool comedian, famous in the UK for his BBC radio show *ITMA (It's That Man Again!)*, which was popular during the Second World War. His programme presented an off-beat, surreal type of humour, introducing such strange characters as Ali Bongo and Mrs. Mopp.

Richard Lindner Artist born in Hamburg, Germany, in 1901, who moved to Paris in 1933 and then to the USA in 1941 to escape Nazi persecution. Originally a concert pianist, he based himself in New York where he received great acclaim, particularly in the fifties for his portrayal of the sordid low life of New York, his often cruel visions of children and the erotic symbolism of his work. Lindner died in 1978. His work most likely appealed to John Lennon.

Albert Einstein One of mankind's greatest examples of genius. Born in West Germany in 1879, he became a noted physicist and was responsible for many major scientific breakthroughs and discoveries, including his most famous: the Theory of Relativity. He spent the last 20 years of his life at the Insititute for Advanced Studies at Princeton and died in 1955.

Simon Rodia Man who designed Watts Towers, an unusual architectural structure of pottery and cement on a steel framework which was completed in 1954. He was also a minor folk artist.

Aleister Crowley British Black magician, known as 'The Great Beast'. He was born in 1875 and was the subject of many scandals. He wrote various books on magical lore and practiced what he called 'Sex Magic'. His philosophy was contained in the phrase: 'Do what thou wilt'. He died in 1947. Rock musician Jimmy Page of Led Zeppelin was to become a Crowley enthusiast, buying first editions of the magician's books – and even the Scottish house in which Crowley had lived for a time.

Wallace Berman A modern painter, based in Los Angeles. Surprisingly, the majority of painters which the Beatles have chosen to include on the *Sgt. Pepper* sleeve are mainly contemporary American artists. There are no modern British artists, such as David Hockney, for instance, or great artists of the past such as Van Gogh. It would be interesting to know the story behind each of the selections.

Larry Bell Contemporary American artist, born in Chicago in 1939. He moved to Little Venice in California and became the leading light in the Los Angeles' art world. From 1964, he turned from painting to concentrate on glass sculpture.

Marlene Dietrich One of the screen's foremost sex goddesses, born in Berlin in 1904, who first made an international impact in 1930 with *The Blue Angel*. She then moved to the USA where her films included *Shanghai Express*, *Destry Rides Again* and *Judgement At Nuremburg*. Dietrich appeared with the Beatles on a Royal Variety Show and one of their favourite Liverpool clubs was called the Blue Angel.

Terry Southern American satirical writer who originally achieved fame in 1958 via a novel *Candy*, a sort of sexy *Candide*, which he co-wrote with Mason Hoffenberg. The novel was originally published by the Olympia Press in Paris and then in the USA, where it became a No. 1 best-seller. Terry Southern also wrote another satirical book, *The Magic Christian*. Ringo Starr appeared in the film versions of both books.

Issy Bonn British music hall and radio star of the forties and early fifities with whom the Beatles probably became familiar through reading the boy's comic *Radio Fun*, which ran a comic strip on Issy Bonn's adventures each week.

Tony Curtis Brooklyn-born Hollywood star who had a great impact on western youth in the fifties – not due to his acting, but to his looks and the famous 'Tony Curtis' haircut. He was later to gain recognition as a talented comedy actor and appeared in the film *Sextette* with Ringo Starr.

Edgar Allen Poe One of America's premier short story writers, also a poet, who was born in 1809. He created the modern detective story and penned many classic short horror tales, such

The characters selected for the cover of the *Pepper* album continue to intrigue – but little is known about who made the selections – and why so many American painters?

as *The Tell-Tale Heart, The Fall Of The House Of Usher* and *The Masque Of The Red Death.* He died in 1949 of a weak heart, caused by drinking too much (in common with Dylan Thomas and W. C. Fields!).

Sir Robert Peel Politician, born in Bury, Lancashire (the same county as the Beatles) in 1788. He became Prime Minister of Great Britain and founded the Conservative Party. He also became noted for repealing the Corn Laws. He died in 1850.

Shirley Temple Hollywood's cutest child star. Born in Santa Monica, California, in 1928, she made her movie debut in *Baby Burkeski* and starred in numerous films, including *Wee Willie*

Winkie and *The Little Princess*, enchanting everyone with her talent, her singing and dancing and her rendition of *The Good Ship Lollipop*. She received a Special Academy Award. Shirley was never able to make the grade as an adult film star and she married and entered politics. As Shirley Temple Black, she devoted her efforts to the Republican Party and was rewarded with an Ambassadorship.

Lewis Carroll Teacher who became a prominent Victorian writer. Born Charles Lutwidge Dodgson in 1832 in Cheshire ('over the water' from Liverpool), most of his fame rested on the magical stories *Alice In Wonderland* and *Through The Looking Glass*. Carroll was one of John Lennon's influences, particularly in the writing of *I Am The Walrus*.

Albert Stubbins Famous footballer from the honourable history of Liverpool FC. Liverpool is internationally famous for its two soccer teams, Liverpool and Everton – although Liverpool remains the legendary side and Stubbins was one of its former heroes.

Tyrone Power Matinee idol and swashbuckling American star who died of a heart attack following a sword fight at the end of the film *Solomon And Sheba*, which had to be completely refilmed with Yul Brynner in the Power role. His other films include *The Eddie Duchin Story, Captain From Castile* and *Son Of Fury*.

Bob Dylan Foremost solo performer of the sixties. He was influenced by the Beatles and they, in turn, were influenced by him. John Lennon, in particular, wrote a couple of numbers under the direct influence of Dylan, a former folk singer, whose articulate lyrics were to gain worldwide appeal. Born Robert Zimmerman in 1941, he changed his surname as a tribute to Welsh poet Dylan Thomas.

Tom Mix Real life 'man of the West' who, after a life as a working cowhand, managed to find employment as a stunt man in Hollywood. He then began to star in Westerns, which were becoming a popular film genre and he was to emerge as one of the most famous Western stars of the silent screen.

Marlon Brando Legendary Hollywood method actor who first rose to fame in a stage portrayal in Tennessee Williams' *A Streetcar Named Desire*, a role in which he made his first major screen appearance. An often controversial figure, his film roles ranged from that of Mark Anthony in *Julius Caesar* to Jor El, Superman's father in *Superman*. His other films include *Mutiny On The Bounty*, *Apocalypse Now*, *The Godfather*, *Last Tango In Paris* and *The Formula*.

T. E. Lawrence Enigmatic hero of the First World War. He united the Arab Nations and led them to fight on behalf of the allies against the Turks, earning the name 'Lawrence Of Arabia'. He was bitterly disappointed that the British did not fulfill their promises to his Arab friends. A mystic, he wrote a number of books, the most famous being *The Seven Pillars Of Wisdom*. He enlisted anonymously in the RAF and died in a motorcycle accident in 1935.

Karl Marx Born in Trier, Germany, in 1818, Marx later moved to England. His experiences among the poverty-stricken people of London's East End caused him to develop a system of social philosophy and, together with Friedrich Engels, he outlined this theory in a pamphlet called *The Communist Manifesto*. It was to have a profound effect on the twentieth-century world and one which he did not anticipate.

Finally, two people of whom information seems quite scarce: **Bobby Breen**, former singer with a British dance band and contemporary American artist **Merkin**.

75 Back In The UK

As the UK did not have a backlog of Beatles' releases, such as those in the USA and Australia, the UK did not boast an all-Beatles Top 5 as in the case of these countries. However, on 7th December 1963, they had a formidable chart presence and the chart positions that week included:

No. 1   *I Want To Hold Your Hand*
No. 2   *She Loves You*
No. 11   *With The Beatles* (LP)
No. 15   *Twist And Shout* (EP)
No. 16   *The Beatles Hits* (EP)
No. 29   *The Beatles No. 1* (EP)

76 That's The Lot

The famous London firm of auctioneers, Sotheby Parke Bernet & Co., began a series of auctions specialising in rock music memorabilia, with the accent on Beatles' material, in 1979.

Here is a list of the twenty highest bids from each of their biggest sales: one on Tuesday 22nd December 1981 and the other on Wednesday 22nd December 1982.

1981

1 £9,900. A piano on which Paul McCartney learned to play and which was sold by his father in 1955. Originally it was anticipated that this item would be sold for between £1,500 and £2,500.

2 £8,800. A self-portrait of John, in pen and ink, portraying his bearded, bespectacled, naked body sitting within a circle, which turns out to be a written message.

3 £8,250. A 1970 Steinway piano, once owned by John Lennon.

4 £5,060. No. 292 of the limited edition of 300 sets of John's 'Bag One' lithographs, complete in the white leather bag which was specially designed by Ted Lapidus.

5 £4,620. 'The Two Virgins'. A perspex and plastic statue of a nude John and Yoko in a pose similar to their *Two Virgins* album sleeve. There were only two made and the sale price of this model, originally believed to be worth between £1,000 and £1,500 was typical of the increased value of collectable Beatle items following John's death.

6 £3,850. A Gold Disc, presented to the Beatles for the album *The Beatles Story*.

7 £3,300. A Harptone guitar which once belonged to George Harrison. It was thought it might bring in from £600 to £900.

8 £2,860. A Raleigh Moped, once owned by John Lennon in the sixties. Originally assessed as being worth between £300 and £500.

9 £2,530. Collarless stage suit once worn by John Lennon, originally thought to be worth between £200 and £300.

Hilary Kay puts another item of Beatles Memorabilia under the hammer.

10   £2,420. Letter written by Paul to a fan when he was appearing at the Star Club in Hamburg. Originally thought to be worth between £180 and £250.

11   £1,870. A Gold Disc presented to the Beatles for the album *Meet The Beatles*.

12   £1,430. A wooden sculpture by John called 'Open And Shut', originally valued at between £250 and £400.

13   £1,320. Large photographic cut-out of Marlene Dietrich, originally used for the *Sgt. Pepper* sleeve. Assessed as being worth between £200 and £300.

14   £1,210. Mounted photographs from the *White Album*, signed by all four members of the Beatles. Originally assessed as being worth between £60 and £100.

15   £1,155. Programme from the Royal Variety Performance with signatures by the Beatles and several other celebrities. Originally valued at between £100 and £150.

16   £1,100. Letter from George Harrison to a girl called Jenny. Written when he was at the Star Club, Hamburg in 1962 and originally estimated to be worth between £150 and £200.

17   £1,045. Letter written by George Harrison to a girl called Jenny.

18   £935. A programme from the premier of *Help!* with a wealth of autographs, including those of John Lennon, Jane Asher, Paul McCartney, Cynthia Lennon, George Harrison and Pattie Boyd.

19   £935. A framed photograph of John Lennon by the famous American photographer Richard Avedon. With Avedon's signature.

20   £935. One of John Lennon's stage jackets from the 1964 period.

The early auctions were very much a testing period to discover what sort of prices Beatles' memorabilia would attract. The largest purchaser in 1981 was Terry Smith, a director of the independent station, Radio City, who spent in excess of £36,000. The material was bought on behalf of the Merseyside museum, Beatle City, which opened in April 1984.

In 1982, the prices were generally much higher, as can be gauged from the following list. The largest purchaser was Kosaku Koishihara, a representative of the Japanese department store, Seibu.

1982

1   £14,300. A Gold Disc originally presented to the Beatles for their *Sgt. Pepper's Lonely Hearts Club Band* album in 1967. Originally estimated as being worth £4,000 to £5,000.

2   £6,050. A mixing console which John used to record his *Imagine* album.

3   £3,300. A large colour collage made by John Lennon in 1966.

4   £3,080. A bronze bust of John by the Royal Academy sculptor K. Carter.

5   £2,420. A pen-and-ink drawing of John Lennon called 'The Motley Bunch'.

6   £2,420. A pen-and-ink drawing by John Lennon called 'The Vicar'.

7   £2,200. A hand-drawn Christmas card which John drew in 1968 using wax crayons.

8   £2,200. George Harrison's stage suit from the 1966 period.

9   £2,200. A felt-tip drawing of himself and Yoko by John Lennon from the year 1969.

10   £1,870. A Gold Disc for *The Beatles Story* album.

11   £1,650. A photocopy of some lyrics from *Gimme Some Truth*, with an extra verse from John.

12   £1,540. A bronze statue by Liverpool artist Alan Curran entitled 'The Beatles In Matthew Street'.

13   £1,430. A black felt-tip drawing by John Lennon entitled 'B'z in his Bonnet or Ants in his Pants'.

14   £1,210 Eight photographs of the Beatles at Aldershot with Pete Best, together with negatives.

15   £1,100. Sixteen photographs from the set of *A Hard Day's Night*, together with negatives.

16   £1,100. Eleven documents concerning John Lennon's trip to Hamburg in 1960.

17   £935. Ten photographs of the Beatles at the Tower Ballroom, New Brighton, together with twenty-two negatives.

18   £935. Handwritten letter to a Cavern fan from John Lennon.

19   £792. Two celluloids from the *Yellow Submarine* film.

20   £770. Three separate items were auctioned at this price: (*a*) a photocopy of lyrics from *One Thing You Can't Hide*, with an additional verse from John; (*b*) John Lennon's original certificate from the Songwriter's Guild (*c*) Gold Disc for Paul McCartney's album *London Town*.

77 Movies Italian Style

Titles of the Beatles' films when released in Italy were:

TUTTI PER UNO: A Hard Day's Night.
AIUTO!: Help!
IL SOTTOMARINO GIALLO: Yellow Submarine
UN GIORNATA CON I BEATLES: Let It Be

78 A Taste Of Trivia – 2

Another selection of fifty items:

1   The entire *Please Please Me* album was recorded in a single day during a marathon 14-hour recording session.

2   Paul McCartney's first single to top both British and American charts since his days with the Beatles was *Ebony And Ivory*.

3   There were over 220,000 applications for the 27,000 seats at the Budo Kan Judo Arena when the Beatles appeared in Japan.

4   *Helter Skelter* was inspired by an article about the Who in *Melody Maker*.

5   At 7 minutes and 11 seconds in length, *Hey Jude* was the lengthiest record to reach No. 1 in the charts up to that time.

6   In October 1964, the Beatles were awarded no less than *five* Ivor Novello Awards for achievements during the previous year.

7   When he lived in Weybridge, Ringo had nine cats and six television sets.

8   Dutch fanzine *Beatles Unlimited* mentions that on Paul McCartney's ode to John Lennon, *Here Today*, the guitar part, when played, goes: D flat, E, A flat, D flat. In other words: D-E-A-D!

9   Only four Beatles' singles failed to reach the No. 1 spot in the UK *Love Me Do*, *Penny Lane*, *Something* and *Let It Be*.

10   Following John's controversial comments about Christ, South Africa (the country which the Beatles had boycotted because of apartheid) banned Beatles' records on the radio until 1971.

11   The *New York Times* described Ringo as: 'the most popular Beatle'.

12   In Linda McCartney's high school yearbook, she was described as: 'a strawberry blonde with a yen for men'.

13   The first Beatles' radio series in the USA was launched by WEEL in Fairfax, Virginia, who began a series of 1-hour programmes each night entitled *Beatles Bonanza*. Both Capitol

Records and Giant Music co-operated in the production of the programme which played Beatles' early hits, discussed merchandising and interviewed visiting Britons.

14 The *Sgt. Pepper* album includes an 8-second track containing such a high-pitched sound that it is only audible to dogs.

15 The name Apple was inspired by the painting by Magritte which hung in Paul McCartney's living room.

16 Will Jordan, the American actor who portrayed TV celebrity Ed Sullivan in the film *I Want To Hold Your Hand,* also appeared as Sullivan in the film *The Buddy Holly Story,* the TV movie *Elvis* and the Broadway play *Elvis-The Legend Lives.*

17 The first Beatles' record to be banned by the BBC was *A Day In The Life,* under the mistaken belief that it was about drugs. The second was *I Am The Walrus,* with its mention of 'knickers'.

18 *Here, There & Everywhere* was inspired by the Beach Boys' song *God Only Knows.*

19 Richard DiLello, 'house hippie' and PR at the Beatles' Apple building and author of *The Longest Cocktail Party,* concerning the Apple venture, was the scriptwriter of the 1983 film *Bad Boys.*

20 Ringo Starr penned the sleeve notes for Count Basie's album *Basie On The Beatles.*

21 Early in 1984, Michael Jackson became the first act in the USA since the Beatles 20 years previously to have seven top singles in a calendar year.

22 To celebrate John's 30th birthday, George wrote the number *It's Johnny's Birthday,* which is featured on the *All Things Must Pass* album set.

23 The original title for *Everybody's Got Something To Hide Except Me and My Monkey* was the much simpler *Come On, Come In.*

24 The first American artist to cover a Beatles' number was Del Shannon with *From Me To You* in 1963.

25 Paul's 39th birthday fell on 18.6.1981, one of the few times in the century when the numbers remain the same when turned upside down. George Martin pointed this out to him.

26 Ringo Starr portrayed the part of Uncle Ernie on the

London Symphony Orchestra's album interpretation of the Who's Rock musical *Tommy*.

27 On the top left hand corner of Wings' *Red Rose Speedway* is a braille message to Stevie Wonder which reads; *We Love You*.

28 The group of vultures in Walt Disney's animated feature of *The Jungle Book* are called John, George, Paul and Ringo.

29 In 1983, the Texas radio station KTST became the first radio station in the world to have a policy of playing records by a single artist only. Their format was altered to play Beatles' music exclusively. Unfortunately, after a year of playing Beatles' records 24 hours a day, they changed into an all-Spanish-speaking station.

30 *With The Beatles* was the first album ever to sell a million copies in the UK.

31 The Monkee's trip to England in 1967 was sponsored by Brian Epstein.

32 The Beatles were No. 1 in the album charts every Christmas from 1963 until 1969 with: *With The Beatles* (1963) *Beatles For Sale* (1964) *Rubber Soul* (1965); *Revolver* (1966); *Sgt. Pepper* (1967); *The Beatles* (1968) and *Abbey Road* (1969).

33 During the making of *The Beatles* double album, Ringo had a furious row with Paul and walked out, not returning for 2 weeks.

34 Yoko Ono and Maureen Starkey are to be heard singing on the chorus of *The Continuing Story Of Bungalow Bill*.

35 Mal Evans was the man who thought up the name Sgt. Pepper's Lonely Hearts Club Band – and he also had a hand in the lyrics. Although he was uncredited, he was given a percentage of the royalties and also contributed lyrics to another of the tracks, *Fixing a Hole*.

36 Paul McCartney's own personal favourite composition is *Here, There And Everywhere*.

37 Yoko Ono is Japanese, George's wife Olivia is Mexican, Ringo's wife Barbara and Paul's wife Linda are American.

38 The very first radio station in the USA to play a Beatles' record on the air was Station WWDC in Washington, DC.

A sensational twosome – Paul and Michael Jackson.

39   Songwriter Jack Lawrence, a friend of Linda McCartney's father Lee Eastman, penned a song about her in 1947 when she was a little girl. Called, simply, *Linda*, it was recorded by Jan and Dean in 1963.

40   In January 1984 when *Pipes Of Peace* was in the No. 1 position in the UK, Paul was also No. 1 in the USA with *Say Say Say*, his duet with Michael Jackson. This was the first time an artist had been No. 1 in both the UK and the USA with a different number since January 1981, when John Lennon held the No. 1 position in the UK with *Imagine* and the No. 1 position in the USA with *(Just Like) Starting Over*.

41   Donovan announced his *Sunshine Superman* hit as 'a song for John and Paul'.

42 During their first major year as a recording band (1963), the Beatles received Gold Discs for *She Loves You* and *I Want To Hold Your Hand*, Silver Albums for *Please Please Me* and *With The Beatles*, a Silver EP for *Twist & Shout* and Silver Discs for *Please Please Me* and *From Me To You*.

43 In The USA, the advance orders of 1,600,000 for *Can't Buy Me Love* created pop history and the record then qualified for a Gold Disc on its official release date, something which had never happened before.

44 An album called *Beatles Barkers* was issued by Passport Records in the USA early in 1984. It consisted of twelve Beatles' numbers sung by a variety of animals including sheep, chickens, dogs and cats.

45 The statue of Eleanor Rigby in Stanley Street, Liverpool was sculpted by Tommy Steele, who appeared with the Beatles on the Royal Variety Show in 1963.

46 Keith Moon died in a London flat owned by Ringo Starr after attending a Paul McCartney 'Buddy Holly' party. It was the same flat where Mama Cass had died.

47 There is only one song which the Beatles recorded on which all four members share songwriting credits; *Flying* which was featured in *Magical Mystery Tour* and on the recordings issued as soundtracks.

48 Because Ringo suffered so many serious illnesses as a child, his grandfather gave him the nickname 'Lazarus'.

49 *Under The Mersey Wall* on George Harrison's *Electronic Sound* album was inspired by a column in the Liverpool Echo called 'Over the Mersey Wall', which was penned by a columnist also called George Harrison.

50 *Sgt. Pepper's Lonely Hearts Club Band* was originally called *Dr. Pepper's Lonely Hearts Club Band* until it was discovered that there was an American soft drink called 'Dr. Pepper's'.

79 The Grammy Awards

At an annual awards ceremony, the American National Academy of Recording Arts and Sciences present their

'Grammy's'. These are the awards which the Beatles received between the years 1964 and 1970:

1964
Best New Artist
Best Vocal Performance By A Group

1966
Song Of The Year   *Michelle*

1967
Best Album   *Sgt. Pepper's Lonely Hearts Club Band*
Best Contemporary Album   *Sgt. Pepper's Lonely Hearts Club Band*
Best Album Cover   *Sgt. Pepper's Lonely Hearts Club Band*
Best Engineered Album   *Sgt. Pepper's Lonely Hearts Club Band*

1969
Best Engineered Recording   *Abbey Road*

1970
Best Original Movie Score   *Let It Be*

80 Some Other Guys

Even before the Beatles entered the recording studios, they had amassed a collection of more than one hundred original songs penned by John and Paul. Once they achieved worldwide fame, there was more than enough self-penned work for them to record. However, there were a number of recordings on which the Beatles performed numbers by other artists, thus sending a healthy amount of royalty payments to the writers of the numbers they admired. Among the non-Lennon & McCartney material which they recorded on original British releases was:

Tracks on *Please Please Me* album:
Anna (Go To Him) Arthur Alexander

Chains Gerry Goffin, Carole King
Boys Luther Dixon, Wes Farrell
Baby It's You Mack David, Burt Bacharach, Barney Williams
A Taste Of Honey Ric Marlow, Bobby Scott
Twist And Shout Bert Burns

Tracks on the *With The Beatles* album:
Till There Was You Meredith Wilson
Please Mr. Postman Brian Holland, Robert Bateman, Berry Gordy
Roll Over Beethoven Chuck Berry
You Really Got A Hold On Me Smokey Robinson
Devil In Her Heart Richard B. Drapkin
Money Janie Bradford, Berry Gordy

Tracks on *Long Tall Sally* EP:
Long Tall Sally Enotris Johnson, Richard Penniman, Robert Blackwell
Slow Down Larry Williams
Matchbox Carl Perkins

Tracks on the *Beatles For Sale* album:
Rock & Roll Music Chuck Berry
Mr Moonlight Roy Lee Johnson
Kansas City Jerry Leiber, Mike Stoller
Hey Hey Hey Richard Penniman
Words Of Love Buddy Holly
Honey Don't Carl Perkins
Everybody's Trying To Be My Baby Carl Perkins

Tracks on the *Help* album:
Dizzy Miss Lizzy Larry Williams
Act Naturally Vonie Morrison, Johnny Russell

Tracks on *A Collection Of Beatle Oldies (But Goodies)* album:
Bad Boy Larry Williams

The above were all 'official' Beatles' releases. The non-Beatles numbers which follow were featured on unofficial recordings, including the Star Club tapes and the Decca Audition material, in addition to appearances made on BBC radio.

Tracks on the albums issued from the *Star Club* tapes:
Hippy Hippy Shake Chan Romero
Sweet Little Sixteen Chuck Berry
Lend Me Your Comb Kay Twomey, Fred Wise, Ben Weisman
Your Feet's Too Big Ada Benson, Fred Fisher
Besame Mucho ConsueloVelzquez
Reminiscing King Curtis
Nothin' Shakin (But The Leaves On The Trees) Cirino Colacrai, Eddie Fontaine, Diane Lampert, Jack Cleveland
To Know Her Is To Love Her Phil Spector
Little Queenie Chuck Berry
Falling In Love Again Sammy Lerner
Be-Bop-A-Lula Gene Vincent, Tex Davis
Hallelujah, I Love Her So Ray Charles
Red Sails In The Sunset Jimmy Kennedy, Will Grosz
I'm Talking About You Chuck Berry
Shimmy Shake Joe South, Billy Land
I Remember You Johnny Mercer, Victor Schertzinger

The Polydor recordings in which they backed Tony Sheridan have been consistently issued on singles and albums over the years. On *My Bonnie, The Saints, Why, Sweet Georgia Brown* and *Nobody's Child*, Sheridan sings lead vocals. However, John Lennon took over lead vocal on:

Ain't She Sweet Jack Yellen, Milton Ager

The Decca Audition tapes have also been issued on various labels:

The Sheik Of Araby Harry Smith, Francis Wheeler, Ed Snyder.
Three Cool Cats Jerry Leiber, Mike Stoller
September In The Rain Al Dubin, Harry Warren
Red Sails In The Sunset Jimmy Kennedy, Will Grosz

Crying, Waiting, Hoping Buddy Holly
Searchin Jerry Leiber, Mike Stoller
Take Good Care Of My Baby Gerry Goffin, Carole King
Sure To Fall (In Love With You) Carl Perkins, Cantrell, Claunch
Memphis, Tennessee Chuck Berry

There were a number of songs performed by the Beatles on various shows which have appeared on a number of bootleg releases. They include:

Beautiful Dreamer Stephen Foster
Carol Chuck Berry
Clarabella Pingatore
Don't Ever Change Gerry Goffin, Carole King
Dream Baby C. Walker
Glad All Over Bennett, Tepper, Schroeder
The Honeymoon Song Theodorakis
I Forgot To Remember To Forget Charlie Feathers, Kesler
I Got A Woman Ray Charles, Richards
I Got To Find My Baby Chuck Berry
I Just Don't Understand Wilkin, Westberry
I'm Gonna Sit Right Down And Cry Thomas, Biggs
I'm Talking About You Chuck Berry
Johnny B. Goode Chuck Berry
Keep Your Hands Off My Baby Gerry Goffin, Carole King
Lonesome Tears In My Eyes Johnny Burnette, D. Burnette, Burlison, Mortimer
Lucille Richard Penniman, Collins
Ooh, My Soul Richard Penniman
A Picture Of You Beveridge, Oakman
A Shot Of Rhythym & Blues Thompson
So How Come (No One Loves Me) Bryant
Soldier Of Love Cason, Moon
That's All Right Mama Arthur Crudup, Elvis Presley
Too Much Monkey Business Chuck Berry
Words Of Love Buddy Holly
Young Blood Jerry Leiber, Mike Stoller, Doc Pomus

81 *Jukebox Jury*

All four members of the Beatles comprised the panel of the BBC TV show *Juke Box Jury* on 7th December 1963 when the programme was filmed from the stage of the Empire Theatre, Liverpool. Of the ten records the Fab Four were asked to comment on, four of them (1, 3, 7, 10) were by Liverpool artists. The records played to the panel were:

1 *I Could Write A Book* The Chants
2 *Kiss Me Quick* Elvis Presley
3 *Hippy Hippy Shake* The Swinging Blue Jeans
4 *Did You Have A Happy Birthday?* Paul Anka
5 *The Nitty Gritty* Shirley Ellis
6 *I Can't Stop Talking About You* Steve Lawrence and Eddie Gorme
7 *Do You Really Love Me Too* Billy Fury
8 *There, I've Said It Again* Bobby Vinton
9 *Love Hit Me* The Orchids
10 *I Think Of You* The Merseybeats

They voted 1, 2, 3, 6, 7 and 10 as hits. The records which actually charted were 2, 3, 7, 8 and 10.

82 Pierian Pearls

The American book company Pierian Press has published more original Beatle books than any other and it has also begun a series of reprints of out-of-print books. Current Beatle titles in their catalogue include:

All Together Now By Harry Castleman and Walter J. Podrazik
The Beatles Again By Harry Castleman and Walter J. Podrazik
Collecting The Beatles By Barbara Fenick
A Day In The Life By Tom Schultheiss

83 Mersey Venues

The Cavern justifiably became known as 'the home of the Beatles', due to the many appearances the group made there. However, there were numerous other venues on Merseyside where the Beatles made appearances. Here is a selection of them:

Liverpool College Of Art Hope Street, The Group were known as 'the college band' and appeared regularly at the art college dances. The Student's Union at the college paid for a PA system which the Beatles could use.

The Casbah Heyman's Green, West Derby. Club run in the cellar of her house by Mrs. Mona Best, mother of Pete Best, who became the Beatles' drummer. It was at this venue that John, Paul and George began to play regularly together.

Wyvern Club Seel Street. This was the club which later became the famous Blue Angel. When it was known as the Wyvern Club, the Silver Beatles, with Stuart Sutcliffe on bass and Johnny Hutchinson on drums, performed an audition for the chance to be Billy Fury's backing group.

The Tower Ballroom New Brighton. The venue has been completely gutted by fire. In the early sixties, the Beatles appeared regularly on big bills on special dances promoted by

164

Sam Leach and Bob Wooler, including an appearance with Little Richard.

Litherland Town Hall Hatton Hill Road. The venue where, on 27th December 1960, the Beatles made their first big impact on Merseyside following a trip to Hamburg. The promoter was Brian Kelly.

Aintree Institute Longmoor Lane. Another popular Brian Kelly venue. Brian booked the Beatles regularly in the early days and was one of the first promoters to recognise their box office potential.

The Jacaranda Club Slater Street. Tiny cellar club run by Alan Williams. The impecunious Beatles couldn't even afford mike stands and their girl friends had to support the mikes on broom handles!

The Plaza Ballroom St. Helens. Ballroom manager Harry Bostock began promoting dances featuring Merseyside groups on a regular basis at the end of the fifties and booked the Beatles on a number of occasions.

Queens Hall Widnes. Impressive venue in the heart of Widnes where NEMS Enterprises featured the Beatles on special gigs in which Brian Epstein increased their local popularity by having them top prestigious bills.

Locarno Ballroom West Derby Road. Liverpool's major Mecca Ballroom. They only rarely booked local bands as dance bands were the main feature at the venues, together with resident beat group, the Delameres. The Beatles most noted gig at the venue took place on St. Valentine's Night, 14th February 1963.

The Pavilion Theatre Lodge Lane. Former music hall. The Beatles appeared as second on the bill to the Royal Show Band from Waterford on 2nd April 1962.

The Majestic Ballroom Conway Street, Birkenhead. The groups here were booked regularly by enterprising ballroom manager Bill Marsden. Due to the fact that there were such large audiences for the Beatles – 500 were turned away one night – Bill introduced the innovation of two separate ballroom shows during the same evening in January 1963.

The Grosvenor Ballroom Grosvenor Street, Wallasey. An early gig for the Silver Beatles on 6th June 1960, when they appeared on a bill with Gerry & The Pacemakers.

New Cabaret Artists A strip club in the Liverpool 8 district run by the ebullient Lord Woodbine where the Beatles provided backing for Janice the Stripper.

The Grafton Ballroom West Derby Road. Liverpool's second Mecca Ballroom. The Beatles made a couple of appearances at this venue – and asked me to be their compere at one of them!

Hambleton Hall St. David's Road, Huyton. Venue where compere Bob Wooler promoted a few gigs. When the Beatles appeared here, he was able to announce to the audience that they had made a record in Hamburg.

The Empire Theatre Lime Street. From their initial appearance on a Carrol Levis *Discoveries* show, they later appeared topping concert bills and also televised their all-Beatles *Juke Box Jury* in December 1963.

The Odd Spot Bold Street. Night club in Liverpool's city centre where the Beatles made three appearances. John's 'step father', John Dykin, worked here.

Civic Hall Ellesmere Port. One of the many venues situated on the banks of the Mersey which featured local bands. The Beatles appeared there on 14th January 1963.

St. Luke's Hall Liverpool Road, Crosby. Hall where promoter Doug Martin presented Mersey groups. It became known as 'The Jive Hive' and the Beatles made a couple of appearances here early in their career.

84 What If?

My list of five items which never happened, but which would have proved of historical importance.

1 *Beatles At The Cavern* A film of the Beatles performing their complete act at the Cavern with announcements by Bob Wooler and interviews with Ray McFall and Cavern regulars.

2 *The Daily Howl* A third published John Lennon book, containing all the stories, poems and drawings he introduced in his Daily Howl exercise books.

3 *The Book Of Liverpool* By Stu Sutcliffe and Bill Harry. A

project I suggested to Stu, with his illustrations of Liverpool in the early sixties, with text written by myself.

4 *Paul's Diary* Eye-witness reports of various Beatles' gigs written in the inimitable style in which Paul wrote several of his reports in *Mersey Beat*.

5 *Ringo's Pictorial History Of The Beatles* Ringo kept taking informal shots of the group with his Pentax camera. A selection of them were printed in a small magazine. A complete portfolio of Ringo's shots tracing the entire career of the Fab Four would have been a welcome addition to Beatle lore.

85 The Mud Slingers

After a suitable pause following John's death, a series of sensationalised accounts of his life were published by various people ranging from his tarot card reader to a former aide. Apart from the 'kiss-and-tell' books, the main source of 'sensationalised' or 'knocking' series on members of the Beatles are to be found in the British tabloids and Sunday newspapers.

Paul McCartney seems the person most vulnerable to these attacks, the first major one coming from George Kelly, a man whom Paul hired as a butler in 1966. After Paul sacked him, Kelly sold his reminiscences to a British Sunday paper, claiming that Paul held drug parties and orgies. Since them, Paul has periodically been the subject of exposés by various people including:

Francie Schwartz A former live-in lover who sold her story to the *News Of The World*, also to *Rolling Stone* magazine and finally revealed all in a book called *Body Count*.

Angie Williams Paul's former stepmother was highly critical of Paul in a series ghosted by former PR man, Tony Barrow, in the *Sun* newspaper. Advertising declared: The startling truth about Paul McCartney. What's it like to be a superstar's poor relation? To be part of the family – but not the fame?'

Ruth McCartney Also ghosted by Tony, in *19* magazine. The least offensive of the 'life among the McCartney's' type articles. Ruth discussed her childhood in the McCartney household.

Jo Jo Laine Denny Laine's ex-wife, pictured in see-through blouses and sexy poses, related a bitchy series of articles in the *Sunday People*, revealing her envy and jealousy of Linda.

Denny Laine The unkindest cut of all. Denny took Paul to pieces in a series published in the *Sun* newspaper, with trailers such as: 'He's mean, mad, moody says old mate Denny Laine' and cruel headlines to stories such as : 'Paul Opted Out Of Dad's Funeral'.

86 *Beatles Unlimited* Checklist

The Dutch fanzine *Beatles Unlimited* is one of the most durable of fanzines and has now passed its fiftieth issue. To give readers an idea of the type of material a fanzine contains, here is a checklist of contents of the first fifty issues:

1   Familiar Dezo Hoffman pose on yellow cover. Features include: 'Abbey Road' (album review); 'George Harrison: Living In The Material World'; 'McGear, Brother On The Run'; 'The Beatles Return To Their Hometown Liverpool'; 'MBE'; 'The Apple Story, Part One'; and 'Dig It' (a bootleg record review column).

2   Four portraits on orange cover. Features include: 'Venus and Mars' (review); 'Live Beatles On Tape'; 'The Apple Story, Part Two'; 'George Harrison's Guitars'; 'Dig It'; 'The John Lennon Horoscope'; 'The Write Thing' (fanzine review); 'Pete Ham of Badfinger'.

3   A still from *Help!* on white cover. Features include: 'How I Won The War'; 'The Apple Story, Part 3'; 'Our Starr' (Fanzine review); 'Tracking The Hits, Part One: Billboard Positions'; 'The Beatles In Holland'.

4   Group portrait on white cover. Features include: 'Wings UK Tour '75'; 'George Harrison 1974'; 'Dig It'; The Fab Four Publication (fanzine review); 'Extra Texture' (review); 'Paul McCartney's Guitars'; 'The Apple Story, Part 4'; 'Ringo 1964'.

5   John Lennon ink portrait on grey cover. Features include: 'Mal Evans' (tribute); 'Wings In Australia'; 'In The Know' (a question and answer column); 'The Cavern'; 'Tracking The Hits, Part 2: The Radio Veronica Positions'; 'With A Little

beatles unlimited

an independent bimonthly for the fans of john, paul, george and ringo

published in the netherlands, p.o. box 602, 3430 ap nieuwegein 49

The Dutch are the most fervent of Beatle fans and the staff of *Beatles Unlimited* are a dedicated band of followers of the Fab Four.

Help From My Friends' (fanzine review); 'Beatles In Germany '66'; 'Dig It'.

6   Paul McCartney picture on green cover. Features include: 'Wings Trip To Holland', Lucky Luxy and Lovely Linda' – a special Wings issue.

7   George Harrison portrait on yellow cover. Features include: 'The Beatles Amps'; 'Tracking The Hits – The Melody Maker Positions'; 'All Together Now' (book review); 'Ringo'; 'In The Know'; 'Beatles Appreciation Society' (fanzine review).

8   Ringo portrait on orange cover. Features include 'A Hard Day's Night, Part 1'; 'Drive My Car'; 'News From The U.K.'; 'A Graphic History'; 'Beatles Discography' (book review); 'Ringo's Drums'; 'The Beatles', White Album Review, Part I'; 'Dig It'.

9   Ringo playing drums on a white cover. Features include: 'U.S. Convention Report'; 'Wings Talk'; 'The First British Beatles Convention'; 'Wings Over California'; 'News From The U.K.'; 'Richard DiLello'; 'August, 1976'; 'Wings In Munich'; 'Dig It'.

10   John Lennon portrait on yellow cover. Features include: 'A Hard Day's Night, Part 2'; 'The First Polish Beatle Gathering'; 'Here, There & Everywhere' (different versions of Beatle songs); 'Beatlemania In Canada'; 'Harrison Alliance', (fanzine review); "John Lennon's Guitars'; 'Magical Mystery Tour '76'; 'Norwich Revisited'; 'News From The U.K.'; 'Dig It'.

11   George Harrison on grey cover. Features include; 'George Harrison Interview'; 'News From The U.K.'; 'We Love You – John And God'; 'Beatlefest '76'; 'Here, There & Everywhere'; 'Thirty Three and a Third' (review); 'Norwegian Wood'; 'Dig It'.

12   John Lennon portrait on green cover. Features include: 'Wings In Sweden, 1972'; 'News From The U.K'; 'I Am The (Boston) Walrus'; 'Here, There & Everywhere'; 'The Beatles White Album, Part 2'; 'Dig It'.

13   Beatles At Hollywood Bowl picture on a yellow cover. Features include: 'Beatles At The Hollywood Bowl;' 'The Beatles Live At The Star Club'; 'News From The U.K.'; 'Klaatu Update'; 'Klaatu' (review).

14   Photograph of Beatles performing on orange cover. Features include: 'All This And World War II' (review); 'Here, There & Everywhere'; 'Tracking The Hits, Part 3: Polish Positions'; 'News From The U.K.'; 'Beatle & Gordon'; 'Life Goes On' (reviews of American albums); 'The German Scene'; 'Germany '76'; 'Dig It'.

15   Portrait of John on blue cover. Features include 'Elvis'; 'Suzy & The Red Stripes'; 'The Beatles In Germany'; 'News From The U.K.'; 'The Dutch Discography'; 'Ringo On TV Commericials'; 'Here, There & Everywhere'; 'Dig It'.

16   Photograph of Beatles around a Christmas tree on a yellow cover. Features include: 'Meet The Staff'; 'The Beatles 1963/4 Christmas Shows'; 'Just Call It Winter Music'.

17   Covers of Beatles Christmas records on grey cover. The entire issue is devoted to reviews of every Beatles' Christmas record.

18   Four pictures of Paul miming on a green cover. Features include: 'Billy J. Kramer & The Dakotas'; 'News From The U.K.'; 'Komm Gib Mir Deine Money'; 'It's Only A Northern Song'; 'Here, There & Everywhere'; 'The Beatles Forever' book review); 'Beatles Information Centre'; 'Who Will Get His Wings'; 'Canada Updated'.

19   Photograph of Ringo and George on a yellow cover. Features include: 'It's Only A Northern Song, part 2'; 'Paul on "London—Town"'; 'Beatlemania' (show review); 'Beatles Information Centre'; 'U.S.A. Updated'; 'I Wanna Hold Your Tambourine, Man'; 'Rutlemania'; 'Beatlefest '78'; 'The Beatles Again' (book review); 'News From The U.K.'; 'Dig It'.

20   Portrait of John on an orange cover. Features include: 'The Butcher Cover'; 'The Dutch Discography'; 'Mersey Beat: The Beginnings Of The Beatles' (book review); 'Ringo O' Records'; 'Here, There & Everywhere'; 'It's Only A Northern Song, Part 3'; 'Israel Updated'; 'Sweden Updated'; 'Wings Tour U.S.A.' (book review); 'News From The U.K.'; 'Dig It'.

20   Photograph of the Fabs posing by a cathedral on a blue cover. Features include: 'The Italian Discography'; 'The Beatles' (book review); 'News From The U.K.'; 'Candy'; 'Beatles Information Centre'; 'The Beatles & The New Wave'; '20 × 4' (bootleg review); 'Canada Updated'.

22   Photograph of Paul on a yellow cover. Features include: 'Sgt. Pepper's Lonely Hearts Club Band' (film review); 'A Twist Of Lennon' (book review); 'Komm Gib Mir Diene Money'; 'Young Blood' (bootleg review); 'Cilla Black'; 'Interesting Facts'; 'Liverpool Beatles Convention'; 'First German Beatles Convention.'

23   Photograph of George on purple cover. Features include: 'The Magic Christian'; 'Behind The Beatles Songs' (book review); 'Interesting Facts'; 'Feedback'; 'You Know My Name, Look Up The Number'; 'Beatles Information Centre'; 'Poland Updated'; 'Here, There & Everywhere'.

24   Photograph of Brian Epstein on green cover. Features include: 'George Harrison's George Harrison'; 'Blindman'; 'Beatles Information Centre'; 'Wings Greatest'; 'The Clive Epstein Interview'; 'Interesting Facts'; 'Xmas Beatle Party'; 'I Read The News Today Oh Boy'; 'Sgt. Pepper's Lonely Hearts Club Band' (the movie); 'The Fifth Dutch Beatles Convention'

25   Previous twenty-four covers on a brown cover. Features include: 'Wings Over The World' (TV review); 'News From The U.K.'; 'Beatles Information Centre'; 'George Harrison In Brazil '79'; 'I Read The News Today Oh Boy'; 'Beatles Conventions'; 'Interesting Facts'; 'Phil Spector'; 'Komm Gib Mir Deine Money'.

26   Portrait of Ringo on orange cover. Features include: 'The Australian Discography'; '200 Motels'; 'Black Or White'; 'Bootleg Reviews'; 'Interesting Facts'; 'I Read The News Today Oh Boy'.

27   Full length photo of the Fabs on a red cover. Features include: 'The Eggtual Interview About Paul's LP'; 'I Read The News Today Oh Boy'; 'Beatles Information Centre'; 'Interesting Facts'; 'Born To Boogie'; 'Good Egg!' 'Beatles Convention News'.

28   Photograph of John on a grey cover. Features include: 'Jimmy McCulloch' (tribute); 'My "Carnival" by Paul McCartney'; 'I Read The News Today Oh Boy'; 'The French Discography'; 'Son Of Dracula' (film review)' 'Komm Gib Mir Deine Money'; 'Deccas Come and Deccas Go(ne)'; 'Bootleg Review'.

29   Group photograph on yellow cover. Features include: 'McCartney; Make A Daft Noise for Christmas?'; 'Interesting Facts'; 'I Read The News Today Oh Boy'; 'Paul Takes Off On Songs Of Wings'; 'Birth Of The Beatles' (film review); 'Maharishi Who Ishi?' 'TM: Transcendental meditation'; 'Sons Of The Beatles'; 'Beatles Information Centre'.

30   Portrait of George on buff cover. Features include: 'Maharishi Who Ishi? Part 2'; 'International Beatles-Dag 1980';

'That'll Be The Day' (film review); 'Beatles Information Centre'; 'I Read The News Today Oh Boy'; 'Interesting Facts'; 'The Beatles Statue Fund'.

31   Group photograph on yellow cover. Features include: 'Life At The Dakota' (book review); 'Every Little Thing' (book review); 'BU's 5th Anniversary'; 'John Lennon "Bag One"'; 'Convention Reports'; 'Beatlemania' (stage show review); 'Dig It'; 'The Concert For The People Of Kampuchea' (review); 'I Read The News Today Oh Boy'; 'Lisztomania' (film review).

32   Photograph of Ringo and Paul in a pram on a brown cover. Features include: 'McCartney II' (review); 'A Day In The Life' (book review)' 'Beatles Concert-Ed Efforts Extra'; 'Interesting Facts'; 'Bert Kaempfert 1923–1980'; 'Beatles Information Centre; I Read The News Today Oh Boy'; 'The Boys From Liverpool' (book review).

33   Photograph of John and Yoko kissing on purple cover. Features include: 'I'm A Loser' (tribute to John); 'I; Me; Mine' (book review); 'Interesting Facts'; 'Double Fantasy' (review); 'I Read The News Today Oh Boy'; What A Bastard The World Is'; 'Peter Sellers'.

34 and 35   Special double issue dedicated to John Lennon with a design drawing on a white cover. Features include: 'John Lennon, A Portrait Of The Artist'; 'I Read The News Today'; 'John Lennon's Death – An Astrological View'; 'Discography'; 'Dig It'; 'Film'; 'Live Appearances'; 'Guest Appearances'; 'New York'; 'When Two Great Saints Meet'; 'USA, East Coast'; 'USA, West Coast'; 'Denmark'; 'Poland'; 'United Kingdom'; 'The Netherlands'; 'Germany'; Sweden.

36   Photograph of Ringo's wedding on a blue cover. 'All Those Years Ago'; 'All You Need Is Ears' (book review); 'I Read The News Today Oh Boy'; 'Yes It Us'; 'Book Reviews'; 'Dig It'.

37   Photograph of Paul playing guitar on yellow cover. 'Beatle Information centre'; 'Somewhere In England' (review). 'I Read The News Today Oh Boy'; 'The Beatles' (book review); 'Caveman' (film review); 'Dig It'.

38   Photographs of the Fab Four in boaters on green cover. Features include: 'I Read The News Today Oh Boy'; 'You Can't Do That' and 'Das Album Der Beatles' (book reviews);

'The Beatles In Italy' (book review); 'Beatles Information Centre'; 'Beatles Liverpool Convention '81'; 'Concert-Ed Efforts Extra'; 'Dig It'.

39   Photograph of John on yellow cover. Features include: 'Mike McGear' (interview); 'The Beatles Information Centre'; 'Beatlefest '81'; 'I Read The News Today Oh Boy'; 'An Uneggspected Television Programme'; 'John Lennon Peace Forest'; 'Interesting Facts'.

40   Photograph of George and Paul on brown cover. Features include: 'Rock And Roll Auction 1981'; 'Beatles Information Centre'; 'The Beatles EP Collection'; 'I Read The News Today Oh Boy'; 'Tribute To John Lennon'; Concert Review; Bootleg Review; 'Dig It'.

41   Photograph of Ringo and John with Brian Epstein on green cover. Features include: 'Beatles Marathon '82'; 'I Read The News Today Oh Boy'; 'The Beatles Radio Activities'; 'The Beatles Collection' (book review); 'Dig It'.

42   Portrait photograph of Paul on orange cover. Features include: 'I Read The News Today Oh Boy'; 'Beatles Information Centre'; 'The Beatles Reel Music' (review) 'The 4Gotten Most'; 'The Beatles, A Collection' and 'As I Write This Letter' (book reviews); 'Beatlefest'; 'Yoko 1981 in Budapest'; 'Interesting Facts'; 'Dig It'.

43 and 44   A special double issue, a 'Beatles Unlimited Special' called 'Lots Of Liverpool', with photographs and maps, a detailed guide to places of interest in Liverpool for Beatle fans.

45   Photograph of Beatles in eskimo suits on red covers. Features include: 'I Read The News Today Oh Boy'; 'Chicago '82'; 'Somewhere In Australia'; 'Home Is Where The Heart Is'; 'The Beatles Australian Singles'; 'Laurence Juber' (interview); 'Dig It'.

46   Portrait photograph of George on a grey cover. Features include: 'I Read The News Today Oh Boy'; 'Pete Best' (interview); 'Bootlegging The Beatles'; 'Beatles Information Centre'; 'A Dark Horse Has Gone Troppo'; 'Dig It'.

47   Photograph of the Fab Four on a white cover. Features include: 'I Read The News Today Oh Boy'; 'Cartoon Beatles'; 'The Ballad of John & Yoko' (book review); 'Abbey Road Revisited'; 'Interesting Facts'; 'Back Into The USSR'; 'Billy

Fury, Mersey Before The Beat'; 'John Lennon's Secret' (book review); 'Beatles Information Centre'; 'Harry Nilsson Interview'; 'Dig It'.

48   Photographic portrait of Ringo on White cover. Features include: 'I Read The News Today Oh Boy'; 'The Albums – 1970 And After'; 'Lennon' (play review); 'Isn't Me Dad Great, Uncle Charlie?'; 'Interesting Facts'; 'Beatles Information Centre'; 'Beatles Radio Activities'; 'Beatles On Record'; 'Beatles Records In Australia'; 'Book Reviews'; 'Dig It'.

49   Photograph of Fab Four on white cover. Features include: 'I Read The News Today Oh Boy'; Amsterdam 83'; 'The Day They Shot John Lennon' (play review); 'Derek Taylor (interview); 'It's Now Or Never'; Beatles at Abbey Road'; 'Dig It'.

50   Photographic portrait of John Lennon on white cover. Features include: 'I Read The News Today Oh Boy'; 'Sotheby's 3rd Auction'; 'Collectin' The Beatles' (book review); 'The Toy Boy'; 'Eric Stewart, Interview' 'Dig It'; 'Interesting Facts'.

87 Seventies Smashes

Despite the demise of the Beatles as a group and the concentration on the solo careers of the individual members of the Fab Four, some Beatles records found their way into the British charts during the seventies when they were reissued. Records by the Beatles which charted in the seventies include:

Let It Be Issued before the parting of the ways. It reached No. 2 in the charts following its release on 14th March 1970.

Yesterday Reached No. 8 in the charts following its release on 13th March 1976.

Hey Jude Reached No. 12 in the charts following its release on 27th March 1976.

Paperback Writer Reached No. 23 in the charts following its release on 27th March 1976.

Penny Lane/Strawberry Fields Forever Reached No. 32 in the charts following its release on 3rd April 1976.

Get Back Reached No. 28 in the charts following its release on 3rd April 1976.

Help! Reached No. 37 in the charts following its release on 10th April 1976.

Back In The USSR Reached No. 19 in the charts following its release on 10th July 1976.

Sgt. Pepper/With A Little Help From My Friends Reached No. 63 in the charts following its release on 7th October 1978.

88 Eighties Hits

At the time of writing, EMI is issuing all of the Beatles' records in sequence exactly 20 years after the originals. Their eighties' hits so far include:

Beatles Movie Medley Reached No. 10 in the charts following its release on 5th June 1982.

Love Me Do Reached No. 4 in the charts following its release on 16th October 1982.

Please Please Me Reached No. 29 in the charts following its release on 22nd January 1983.

From Me To You Reached No. 40 in the charts following its release on 23rd April 1983.

She Loves You Reached No. 45 in the charts following its release on 3rd September 1983.

I Want To Hold Your Hand Reached No. 62 in the charts following its release on 26th November 1983.

Can't Buy Me Love Reached No. 52 in the charts following its release on 31st March 1984.

89 Movie Medley

The Beatles Movie Medley was the record which provided the Beatles with their first entry into the singles charts of the eighties and was issued on 5th June 1982, almost exactly 20 years since their first recording audition with George Martin on 6th June 1962.

A short career on the silver screen resulted in some further musical gems.

The segue single comprised excerpts from the following previously released Beatles' records:

Magical Mystery Tour
All You Need Is Love
You've Got To Hide Your Love Away
I Should Have Known Better
A Hard Day's Night
Ticket To Ride
Get Back

90 George's Solo Years

George's albums and singles.

ALBUMS

Wonderwall Music (1st November 1968) Tracks: *Microbes; Red Lady Too; Tabla And Pakavaj; In The Park; Drilling A Home; Guru Vandana; Greasy Legs; Ski-Ing; Gat Kirwani; Dream Scene; Party Secombe; Love Scene; Crying; Cowboy Music; Fantasy Sequins; On The Bed; Glass Box; Wonderwall To Be Here; Singing Om.*

Electronic Sound (9th May 1969) Tracks: *Under The Mersey Wall; No Time Or Space.*

All Things Must Pass (27th November 1970) Tracks: *I'd Have You Anytime; My Sweet Lord; Wah-Wah; Isn't It A Pity; What Is Life; If Not For You; Behind That Locked Door; Let It Down; Run Of The Mill; Beware Of Darkness; Apple Scruffs; Ballad Of Sir Frankie Crisp (Let It Roll); Awaiting On You All; All Things Must Pass; I Dig Love; Art Of Dying; Isn't It A Pity; Hear Me Lord; Out Of The Blue; It's Johnny's Birthday; Plug Me In; I Remember Jeep; Thanks For The Pepperoni.*

The Concert For Bangla Desh (7th January 1972) With various artists. Tracks: *Bangla Dhun; Wah-Wah; My Sweet Lord; Awaiting On You All; That's The Way God Planned It; It Don't Come Easy; Beware Of Darkness; While My Guitar Gently Weeps; Jumpin' Jack Flash/Young Blood; Here Comes The Sun; A Hard Rain's Gonna Fall; It Takes A Lot To Laugh/It Takes A Train To Cry; Blowin' In The Wind; Mr. Tambourine Man; Just Like A Woman; Something; Bangla Desh.*

Living In The Material World (21st June 1973) Tracks: *Give Me Love (Give Me Peace On Earth); Sue Me Sue You Blues; The Light That Has Lighted The World; Don't Let Me Wait Too Long; Who Can See It; Living In The Material World; The Lord Loves The One (That Loves The Lord); Be Here Now; Try Some Buy Some; The Day The World Gets 'Round; That Is All.*

Now that he's retired from recording, there are likely to be no further releases from George . . . but we can always live in hope.

Dark Horse (20th December 1974)
Tracks: *Hari's On Tour (Express); Simply Shady; So Sad; Bye*

Bye Love; Maya Love; Ding Dong Ding Dong; Dark Horse; Far East Man; It Is 'He'.

Extra Texture (Read All About It) (9th September 1975)
Tracks: *You; The Answer's At The End; This Guitar (Can't Keep From Crying); Ooh Baby (You Know That I Love You); World Of Stone; A Bit More Of You; Can't Stop Thinking About You; Tired Of Midnight Blue; Grey Cloudy Lies; His Name Is Legs (Ladies And Gentlemen).*

Thirty Three And A $\frac{1}{3}$ (19th November 1976)
Tracks: *Women Don't You Cry For Me; Dear One; Beautiful Girl; This Song; See Yourself; It's What You Value; True Love; Pure Smokey; Crackerbox Palace; Learning How To Love You.*

The Best Of George Harrison (20th November 1976)
Tracks: *Something; If I Needed Someone; Here Comes The Sun; Taxman; Think For Yourself; For You Blue; While My Guitar Gently Weeps; My Sweet Lord; Give Me Love (Give Me Peace On Earth); You; Bangla Desh; Dark Horse; What Is Life.*

George Harrison (23rd Febarury 1979)
Tracks: *Love Comes To Everyone; Not Guilty; Here Comes The Moon; Soft-Hearted Hana; Blow Away; Faster; Dark Sweet Lady; Your Love Is Forever; Soft Touch; If You Believe.*

Dark Horse (27th November 1980)
Tracks: as previously mentioned.

Somewhere In England (5th June 1981)
Tracks: *Blood From A Clone; Unconsciousness Rules; Life Itself; All Those Years Ago; Baltimore Oriole; Teardrops; That Which I Have Lost; Writing's on The Wall; Hong Kong Blues; Save The World.*

Gone Troppo (8th November 1982)
Tracks: *Wake Up My Love; That's The Way It Goes; I Really Love You; Greece; Mystical One; Baby Don't Run Away; Dream Away; Circles.*

SINGLES
My Sweet Lord c/w *What Is Life* (15th January 1971)
Bangla Desh c/w *Deep Blue* (30th July 1971)
Give Me Love (Give Me Peace On Earth) c/w *Miss O'Dell* (25th May 1973)
Ding Dong c/w *I Don't Care Anymore* (6th December 1974)

Dark Horse c/w *Hari's On Tour (Express)* (28th February 1975)

You c/w *World Of Stone* (12th September 1975)

This Guitar (Can't Keep From Crying) c/w *Maya Love* (6th February 1976)

This Song c/w *Learning How To Love You* (19th November 1976)

My Sweet Lord c/w *That Is Life* (1976 December)

True Love c/w *Pure Smokey* (18th February 1977)

It's What You Value c/w *Woman Don't You Cry For Me* (10th June 1977)

Blow Away c/w *Soft Touch* (2nd March 1979)

Love Comes To Everyone c/w *Soft Hearted Hana* (1979 May)

Faster c/w *Your Love Is Forever* (20th July 1979)

All Those Years Ago c/w *Writing's On The Wall* (16th May 1981)

Teardrops c/w *Save The World* (31st July 1981)

Wake Up My Love c/w *Greece* (8th November 1982)

91 Ringo's Solo Years

Ringo's albums and singles.

ALBUMS

Sentimental Journey (27th March 1970)
Tracks: *Sentimental Journey; Night And Day; Whispering Grass (Don't Tell The Trees); Bye Bye Blackbird; I'm A Fool To Care; Star Dust; Blue Turning Grey Over You; Love Is A Many Splendoured Thing; Dream; You Always Hurt The One You Love; Have I Told You Lately That I Love You; Let The Rest Of The World Go By.*

Beaucoups Of Blues (25th September 1970)
Tracks: *Beaucoups Of Blues; Love Don't Last Long; Fastest Growing Heartache In The West; Without Her; Woman Of The Night; I'd Be Talking All The Time; $ D5 Draw; Wine, Women and Loud, Happy Songs; I Wouldn't Have You Any Other Way; Loser's Lounge; Waiting; Silent Homecoming.*

Ringo (9th November 1973)

Tracks: *I'm The Greatest; Have You Seen My Baby; Photograph; Sunshine Life For Me (Sail Away Raymond); You're Sixteen; Oh My My; Step Lightly; Six O'Clock; Devil Woman; You and Me (Babe).*

Goodnight Vienna (15th November 1974)
Tracks: *Goodnight Vienna; Occapella; Oo-Wee; Husbands And Wives; Snookeroo; All By Myself; Call Me; No No Song; Only You; Easy For Me; Goodnight Vienna (Reprise).*

Blast From Your Past (12th December 1975)
Tracks: *You're Sixteen; No No Song; It Don't Come Easy; Photograph; Back Off Boogaloo; Only You (And You Alone); Beaucoups Of Blues; Oh My My; Early 1970; I'm The Greatest.*

Ringo's Rotogravure (17th September 1976)
Tracks: *A Dose Of Rock 'n' Roll; Hey Baby; Pure Gold; Cryin'; You Don't Know Me At All; Cookin' (In The Kitchen Of Love); I'll Still Love You; This Be Called A Song; Las Brisas; Lady Gaye; Spooky Weirdness.*

Ringo The 4th (30th September 1977)
Tracks: *Drowning In The Sea Of Love; Tango All Night; Wings; Gave It All Up; Out On The Streets; Can She Do It Like She Dances; Sneaking Sally Through The Alley; It's No Secret; Gypsies In Flight; Simple Love Song.*

Bad Boy (June 1978)
Tracks: *Who Needs A Heart; Bad Boy; Lipstick Traces (On A Cigarette); Heart On My Sleeve; Where Did Our Love Go; Hard Times; Tonight; Monkey See-Monkey Do; Old Time Relovin'; A Man Like Me.*

Ringo (27th November 1980)
Tracks: as previously mentioned.

Stop and Smell The Roses (20th November 1981)
Tracks: *Private Property; Wrack My Brain; Drumming Is My Madness; Attention; Stop And Take The Time To Smell The Roses; Dead Giveaway; You Belong To Me; Sure To Fall (In Love With You); Nice Way; Back Off Boogaloo.*

Blast From Your Past (25th November 1981)
Tracks: as previously mentioned.

Old Wave (24th June 1983)
Tracks: *She's About A Mover; Everybody's In A Hurry But Me; Alibi; I Keep Forgettin'; In My Car; Hopeless; Be My Baby; As*

Far As We Can Go; Picture Show Life; Going Down.

SINGLES
It Don't Come Easy c/w *Early 1970* (9th April 1971)
Back Off Boogaloo c/w *Blindman* (17th March 1972)
You're Sixteen c/w *Devil Woman* (8th February 1974)
Only You (And You Alone) c/w *Call Me.* (15th November 1974)
Snookeroo c/w *Oo-Wee* (21st February 1975)
Oh My My c/w *No No Song* (9th January 1976)
A Dose Of Rock 'n' Roll c/w *Cryin'* (15th October 1976)
Hey Baby c/w *Lady Gaye* (26th November 1976)
Tonight c/w *Heart On My Sleeve* (21st July 1978)
Wrack My Brain c/w *Drumming Is My Madness* (13th November 1981)

92 Paul's Solo Years

Paul's albums and singles.

ALBUMS
  McCartney (17th April 1970)
Tracks: *The Lovely Linda; That Would Be Something; Valentine Day; Every Night; Hot As Sun; Glasses; Junk; Man We Was Lonely; Oh You; Momma Miss America; Teddy Boy; Singalong Junk; Maybe I'm Amazed; Kreen-Akore.*
  Ram (21st May 1971)
Tracks: *Too Many People; 3 Legs; Ram On; Dear Boy; Uncle Albert/Admiral Halsey; Smile Away; Heart Of The Country; Monkberry Moon Delight; Eat At Home; Long Haired Lady; Ram On; The Back Seat Of My Car.*
  Wild Life (3rd December 1971)
Tracks: *Mumbo; Bip Bop; Love Is Strange; Wild Life; Some People Never Know; I Am Your Singer; Tomorrow; Dear Friend.*
  Red Rose Speedway (3rd May 1973)
Tracks: *Big Barn Bed; My Love; Get On The Right Thing; One More Kiss; Little Lamb Dragonfly; Single Person; When The*

Night; Loup (1st Indian On The Moon); Hold Me Tight; Lazy Dynamite; Hands Of Love; Power Cut.

Band On The Run (30th November 1979)

Tracks: *'Band' On The Run; Jet; Bluebird; Mrs. Vanderbilt; Let Me Roll It; Mamunia; No Words; Picasso's Last Words (Drink To Me); Nineteen Hundred and Eighty Five.*

Venus & Mars (30th May 1975)

Tracks: *Venus & Mars; Rock Show; Love In Song; You Gave Me The Answer; Magneto And Titanium Man; Letting Go; Venus And Mars Reprise; Spirits Of Ancient Egypt; Medicine Jar; Call Me Back Again; Listen To What the Man Said; Treat Her Gently; Lonely Old People; Crossroads Theme.*

Wings At The Speed Of Sound (26th March 1976)

Tracks: *Let 'Em In; The Note You Never Wrote; She's My Baby; Beware My Love; Wino Junko; Silly Love Songs; Cook Of The House; Time To Hide; Must Do Something About It; San Ferry Anne; Warm And Beautiful.*

Wings Over America (10th December 1976)

Tracks: *Venus & Mars; Rock Show; Jet; Let Me Roll It; Spirits Of Ancient Egypt; Medicine Jar; Maybe I'm Amazed; Call Me Back Again; Lady Madonna; The Long And Winding Road; Live And Let Die; Picasso's Last Words; Richard Cory; Bluebird; I've Just Seen A Face; Blackbird; Yesterday; You Gave Me The Answer; Magneto And Titanium Man; Go Now; My Love; Listen To What The Man Said; Let 'Em In; Time To Hide; Silly Love Songs; Beware My Love; Letting Go; Band On The Run; Hi, Hi, Hi; Soily.*

London Town (31st March 1978)

Tracks: *London Town; Cafe On The Left Bank; I'm Carrying; Backwards Traveller; Cuff Link; Children Children; Girlfriend; I've Had Enough; With A Little Luck; Famous Groupies; Deliver Your Children; Name And Address; Don't Let It Bring You Down; Mouse Moose And The Grey Goose.*

Wings Greatest (1st December 1978)

Tracks: *Another Day; Silly Love Songs; Live And Let Die; Junior's Farm; With A Little Luck; Band On The Run; Uncle Albert/Admiral Halsey.*

Back To The Egg (8th June 1979)

Tracks: *Reception; Getting Closer; We're Open Tonight; Spin It*

Paul has had more singles issued than any of the other ex-members of the Beatles.

On; Again And Again And Again; Old Siam Sir; Arrow Through Me; Rockestra Theme; To You; After The Ball; Million Miles; Winter Rose; Love Awake; The Broadcast; So Glad To See You Here; Baby's Request.
  McCartney II (16th May 1980)
Tracks: *Coming Up; Temporary Secretary; On The Way; Water-*

falls; Nobody Knows; Front Parlour; Summers Day Song; Frozen Jap; Bogey Music; Darkroom; One Of These Days.

The McCartney Interview (23rd February 1981)

Tug Of War (26th April 1982)

Tracks: *Tug Of War; Take It Away; Somebody Who Cares; What's That You're Doing; Here Today; Ballroom Dancing; The Pound Is Sinking; Wanderlust; Get It; Be What You See; Dress Me Up As A Robber; Ebony And Ivory.*

Pipes Of Peace (31st October 1983)

Tracks: *Pipes Of Peace; Say Say Say; The Other Me; Keep Under Cover; So Bad; The Man; Sweetest Little Show; Average Person; Hey Hey; Through Our Love.*

Give My Regards to Broad Street (October 1984)

Tracks: *No More Lonely Nights; Good Day Sunshine; Corridor Music; Yesterday; Here, There And Everywhere; Wanderlust; Ballroom Dancing; Silly Love Songs; Not Such A Bad Boy; No Values; For No-One; Eleanor Rigby; Eleanor's Dream; Long And Winding Road.*

SINGLES

Another Day c/w *Oh Woman Oh Why* (18th February 1971)

The Back Seat Of My Car c/w *Heart Of The Country* (13th August 1971)

Give Ireland Back To The Irish c/w *Give Ireland Back To The Irish* (25th February 1972)

Mary Had A Little Lamb c/w *Little Woman Love.* (5th May 1972)

My Love c/w *The Mess* (23rd March 1973)

Live And Let Die c/w *I Lie Around* (1st June 1973)

Helen Wheels c/w *Country Dreamer* (26th October 1973)

Jet c/w *Let Me Roll It* (18th February 1974)

Band On The Run c/w *Zoo Gang* (28th June 1974)

Walking In The Park With Eloise c/w *Bridge Over The River Suite* (18th October 1974)

Junior's Farm c/w *Sally G* (25th October 1974)

Listen To What The Man Said c/w *Love In Song* (16th May 1975)

Letting Go c/w *You Gave Me The Answer* (5th September 1975)

Venus & Mars/Rock Show c/w *Magneto And Titanium Man* (28th November 1975)
Silly Love Songs c/w *Cook Of The House* (30th April 1976)
Let 'Em In c/w *Beware My Love* (23rd July 1976)
Maybe I'm Amazed c/w *Soily* (4th February 1977)
Mull Of Kintyre c/w *Girls School* (11th November 1977)
With A Little Luck c/w *Backwards Traveller/Cuff Link* (23rd March 1978)
I've Had Enough c/w *Deliver Your Children* (16th June 1978)
London Town c/w *I'm Crying* (15th September 1978)
Goodnight Tonight c/w *Daytime Nightime Suffering* (23rd March 1978)
Old Siam Sir c/w *Spin It On* (1st June 1979)
Getting Closer c/w *Baby's Request* (10th August 1979)
Wonderful Christmastime c/w *Rudolph The Red Nosed Reggae* (16th November 1979)
Coming Up c/w *Lunchbox/Odd Sox* (11th April 1980)
Waterfalls c/w *Check My Machine* (14th June 1980)
Temporary Secretary c/w *Secret Friend* (15th September 1980)
Ebony And Ivory c/w *Rainclouds* (29th March 1982)
Take It Away c/w *I'll Give You A Ring* (21st June 1982)
The Girl Is Mine c/w *Can't Get Out Of The Rain* (28th November 1982)
Say Say Say c/w *Ode To A Koala Bear* (3rd October 1983)
Pipes Of Peace c/w *So Bad* (5th December 1983)
No More Lonely Nights c/w *Silly Love Songs* (1984)

93 John's Solo Years

John's albums and singles.

ALBUMS

Unfinished Music No. 1 – Two Virgins (29th November 1968)
Tracks: *Two Virgins I; Together; Two Virgins 2; Two Virgins 3; Two Virgins 4; Two Virgins 5; Two Virgins 6; Hushabye, Hushabye; Two Virgins 7; Two Virgins 8; Two Virgins 9; Two Virgins 10.*

Unfinished Music No. 2 – Life With The Lions (9th May 1969)

Tracks: *Cambridge 1969; No Bed For Beatle John; Baby's Heartbeat; Two Minute's Silence; Radio Play.*

The Wedding Album (7th November 1969)

Tracks: *John And Yoko; Amsterdam.*

The Plastic Ono Band – Live Peace In Toronto 1969 (12th December 1969)

Tracks: *Blue Suede Shoes; Money; Dizzy Miss Lizzy; Yer Blues; Cold Turkey; Give Peace A Chance; Don't Worry Kyoko (Mummy's Only Looking For A Hand In The Snow); John John (Let's Hope For Peace).*

John Lennon/Plastic Ono Band (11th December 1970)

Tracks: *Mother; Hold On; I Found Out; Working Class Hero; Isolation; Remember; Love; Well Well Well; Look At Me; God; My Mummy's Dead.*

Imagine (8th October 1971)

Tracks: *Imagine; Crippled Inside; Jealous Guy; It's So Hard; I Don't Want To Be A Soldier Mama, I Don't Want To Die; Give Me Some Truth; Oh My Love; How Do You Sleep?; How; Oh Yoko.*

Some Time In New York City (15th September 1972)

Tracks: *Woman Is The Nigger Of The World; Sisters O Sisters; Attica State; Born In A Prison; New York City; Sunday Bloody Sunday; The Luck Of The Irish; John Sinclair; Angela; We're All Water; Cold Turkey; Don't Worry Kyoko; Well (Baby Please Don't Go); Jamrag; Scumbag; AU.*

Mind Games (16th November 1973)

Tracks: *Mind Games; Tight A$; Aisumasen (I'm Sorry); One Day (At A Time); Bring On The Lucie (Freda Peeple); Nutopian National anthem; Intuition; Out Of The Blue; Only People; I Know (I Know); You Are Here; Meat City.*

Walls And Bridges (4th October 1974)

Tracks: *Going Down On Love; Whatever Gets You Thru The Night; Old Dirt Road; What You Got; Bless You; Scared; No. 9 Dream; Surprise Surprise (Sweet Bird Of Paradox); Steel And Glass; Beef Jerky; Nobody Loves You (When You're Down and Out); Ya Ya.*

Rock 'N' Roll (21st February 1975)

Tracks: *Be-Bop-A-Lula; Stand By Me; Rip It Up/Ready Teddy; You Can't Catch Me; Ain't That A Shame; Do You Wanna*

Sadly, no more Lennon masterpieces will be coming our way.

Dance; Sweet Little Sixteen; Slipping and Slidin; Peggy Sue Bring It On Home To Me/Send Me Some Lovin'; Bony Moronie; Ya Ya; Just Because.

Shaved Fish (Collectable Lennon) (24th October 1975)

Tracks: *Give Peace A Chance; Cold Turkey; Instant Karma; Power To The People; Mother; Woman Is The Nigger Of The World; Imagine; Whatever Gets You Thru The Night; Mind Games; No. 9. Dream; Happy Xmas (War Is Over); Give Peace A Chance.*

Double Fantasy (17th November 1980)
Tracks: *(Just Like) Starting Over; Kiss Kiss Kiss; Clean Up Time; Give Me Something; I'm Losing You; I'm Moving On; Beautiful Boy (Darling Boy); Watching The Wheels; I'm Your Angel; Woman; Beautiful Boys; Dear Yoko; Every Man Has A Woman Who Loves Him; Hard Times Are Over.*

Mind Games (27 November 1980)
Tracks: as previously mentioned.

Rock 'N' Roll (25th November 1981)
Tracks: as previously mentioned.

The John Lennon Collection (8th November 1982)
Tracks: *Give Peace A Chance; Instant Karma; Power To The People; Whatever Gets You Thru The Night; No. 9. Dream; Mind Games; Love; Happy Xmas (War Is Over); Imagine; Jealous Guy; Stand By Me; (Just Like) Starting Over; Woman; I'm Losing You; Beautiful Boy (Darling Boy); Watching The Wheels; Dear Yoko.*

Heartplay – An Unfinished Dialogue (16th December 1983)
Excerpts from the interviews conducted for *Playboy* magazine.

Milk And Honey (23rd January 1984)
Tracks: *I'm Stepping Out; O Sanity; I Don't Wanna Face It; Don't Be Scared; Nobody Told Me; Borrowed Time; Your Hands; (Forgive Me) My Little Flower Princess; Let Me Count The Ways; Grow Old With Me; You're The One.*

SINGLES
Give Peace A Chance c/w *Remember Love* (4th July 1969)
Cold Turkey c/w *Don't Worry Kyoko (Mummy's Only Looking For A Hand In The Snow* (24th October 1969)
Instant Karma c/w *Who Has Seen The Wind* (6th February 1970)
Power To The People c/w *Open Your Box* (12th March 1971)
Happy Xmas (War Is Over) c/w *Listen The Snow Is Falling* (24th November 1972)

190

Mind Games c/w *Meat City* (16th November 1973)
Whatever Gets You Thru The Night c/w *Beef Jerky* (4th October 1974)
No. 9. Dream c/w *What You Got* (31st January 1975)
Stand By Me c/w *Move Over Ms. L.* (18th April 1975)
Imagine c/w *Working Class Hero* (24th October 1975)
Just Like Starting Over c/w *Kiss Kiss Kiss* (24th October 1980)
Woman c/w *Beautiful Boys* (16th January 1981)
Watching The Wheels c/w *Yes I'm Your Angel* (27th March 1981)
Love c/w *Give Me Some Truth* (15th November 1982)
Nobody Told Me c/w *O Sanity* (9th January 1984)
Borrowed Time c/w *Your Hands* (9th March 1984)
Stepping Out c/w *Sleepless Night* (9th July 1984)

94 The Stage Is Set

There have been a number of stage plays presenting either the Beatles' story or, simply, the Beatles' music performed by other artists. Here is a selection of twelve such shows:

1   *Beatlemania* Stage show produced by Stephen Leber at the Winter Gardens Theatre, Broadway, New York. Actors included Joe Pecorrino as John, Leslie Fradkin as George and Justin McNeal as Ringo. The Beatles considered legal action and their representative John Eastman commented: 'I'm representing all four and they are very angry at this show. They have been ripped off. These guys have just taken someone else's act and recreated it completely'. The show proved to be very successful and there was a film version, a touring show and presentations in several countries including Japan, the UK and South America.

2   *A Day In The Life* a stage review by Libby Adler Mages and Daniel Golman, based on Lennon & McCartney compositions, which the authors intended to present in a number of American cities during 1984.

3   *The Day They Shot John Lennon* Dramatic play which

opened for a short season at the N.J. Theatre, Princeton, in the USA in January 1983. The play was penned by James McLure.

4 *In His Own Write* Play penned by Adrienne Kennedy and Victor Spinetti, based on John's two books. originally performed in December 1967 in a single performance, the play, directed by Victor Spinetti, opened at the Old Vic Theatre, London, on 18th June 1968. John and Yoko attended the first night. The main character in the drama was called 'Me', a chap born on the same day as John himself.

5 *In His Own Write* A one-man show which ran at the Lyric Theatre, Hammersmith, for a month during January 1982. Entrance was £1 and all performances took place in the afternoon. Man on the stage was actor Gareth Williams, who put on the show together with director Michael Matz. There were only a few props, some funny hats and a number of slides of John's drawings were shown. Williams recited excerpts from John's two books, also quoted from various interviews which had been conducted with John and sang *Instant Karma, Working Class Hero* and *Imagine*.

6 *Imagine* Another tribute to John Lennon. This time a musical based on John's Life and featuring his songs. The review was presented by Abbey Road Productions at the Colonial Tavern, Toronto, Canada, in May 1981.

7 *John, Paul, George, Ringo . . . and Bert* The first real stage play about the Beatles, penned by Liverpool writer, Willie Russell, and originally staged in Liverpool, before moving to the Lyric Theatre, Hammersmith, and then on to the West End in 1976, where it won the *Evening Standard* Award as Best Comedy of the Year. The musical was revived in 1983 when it was presented at the Old Vic in August. The basic story tells the details of the Fab Four's rise to fame, their eventual disintegration, all related to the audience by a young admirer, Bert.

8 *Lennon* Musical, originally launched at the Everyman Theatre in Liverpool on 28th October 1981, which later moved to New York. Written by Bob Eaton, who also directed the play, it was based on various interviews which Eaton conducted with people such as Alan Williams and Tony Barrow and featured several Mersey actors who had several roles to play. At a later stage in its development, the rights to the play were

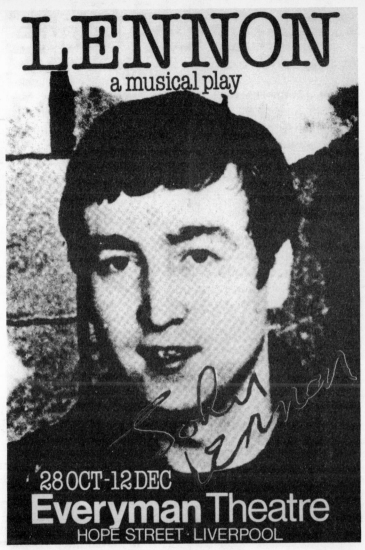

LENNON
a musical play

28 OCT - 12 DEC
Everyman Theatre
HOPE STREET · LIVERPOOL

Liverpool saw the premier of *John, Paul, George, Ringo . . . And Bert*
and the *Lennon* play. The latest Mersey play to open in Liverpool was
Cellar of Dreams, Spencer Leigh's play about the Cavern which began
a short season from August 1984.

193

acquired by Clive Epstein and Syd Bernstein and later resold to an organisation which presented the play in New York.

9 *Lucy In The Sky* A rock-opera devised by Michael Bogdanov, who directed the production. Based on the *Sgt. Pepper's Lonely Hearts Club Band* album, the show was originally presented at the Phoenix Theatre, Leicester between 12th May and 18th June 1977, prior to a 6-week tour of Hull, Leeds, Harlow and Croydon. Bogdanov was theatre director at Leicester and music arrangements were done by the Phoenix Theatre Company. The opera included circus acts and was presented in a marquee erected in the car park adjacent to the theatre.

10 *Sgt. Pepper's Lonely Hearts Club Band On The Road* Theatre show, directed by Tom O'Horgan and produced by Robert Stigwood, launched as a major musical production at the Beacon Theatre, New York, on 14th November 1974. John Lennon actually turned up at the premier and gave the show his blessing, despite the fact that the Beatles generally attempted to sue and request injunctions against such use of their material. Stigwood was to turn *Sgt. Pepper* into a multi-million dollar movie flop.

11 *Stu* Subtitled 'Scenes from the life of Stuart Sutcliffe', a play by Jeremy Stockwell and Hugh O'Neill which was presented at the Bromley Little Theatre, London, from 21st–24th September 1983. The late Mrs. Sutcliffe and her daughter Pauline attended the opening. There was only one actor in the play, Paul Almost, who portrayed Stu.

12 *With A Little Help From My Friends* West End show which opened at the Duke of York Theatre in St. Martin's Lane, London on 28th July 1981. The show was presented by Terry Francis and Barry Stacey and was a 2-hour entertainment in which four singers sang thirty Beatles' songs, with Paul Burton relating the story of the Fab Four. Jacqueline Reddin and Janet Shaw were the two female singers and Steve Devereux and Michael Heath the males. The show closed after a single week. Jacqueline, who was then to take over the lead in the stage version of *Grease*, commented: 'The whole thing was a disaster. We had to learn thirty-six songs and the choreography in 2 weeks. There just wasn't enough time'.

95 Liverpool 1984

For Beatles buffs, 1984 was the most exciting year since the city held the Civic Reception in 1964. Here are ten of the places of interest found in Liverpool during the year:

1 *The Atlantic Tower Hotel* New hotel in Chapel Street which offers special 'Beatles' Weekends', including a Beatles' disco, films, local tours, guest speakers and a sixties' ball. There is a statue of John Lennon in the foyer and McCartney's bistro has a Beatles' menu (see List 106).

2 *Beatle City* The £2,000,000 multi-media complex, opened by Radio City and Merseyside County Council in Seel Street in April. A trip through the Beatles' history in a unique presentation with a miniature Cavern, film studios, memories of Hamburg, a recreation of Brian Epstein's office and a display of memorabilia, including Ringo's car. Also a place for Beatle fans to meet and relax with a souvenir shop and coffee bar.

3 *The Beatles Shop* A new souvenir shop situated directly opposite the rebuilt Cavern in Mathew Street. The owners also unveiled a Beatles' statue in April 1984.

4 *Beatle Streets* Opened in 1981 as part of a new estate near West Derby Road in Liverpool 6, they comprise John Lennon Drive, Paul McCartney Way, George Harrison Close and Ringo Starr Drive.

5 *Cavern Mecca* Liverpool's original Beatles' museum, launched in the seventies by Liz and Jim Hughes, also known as the Beatles' Information Centre. It moved to No. 9 Dream, Cavern Walks, Mathew Street in April 1984. Memorabilia, souvenirs and a meeting place for all genuine Beatle fans.

6 *Cavern Walks* A £9,000,000 complex, designed by architect David Backhouse and officially opened in Mathew Street on 26th April a few weeks following the opening of Beatle City. A £75,000 statue of the Fab Four was unveiled by Mike McCartney on Cavern Walks, the Cavern Mecca found a new home in the building and a rebuilt Cavern Club was opened with a show featuring the Swinging Blue Jeans, the Merseybeats and Billy J. Kramer.

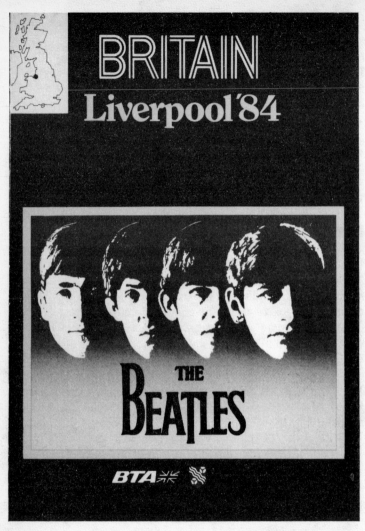

Twenty years on and the Mersey Beat sound is still popular with record collectors.

7 *Eleanor Rigby* Although unveiled a few years previously, visitors in 1984 were tickled pink with this intriguing little sculpture sitting on a bench in Stanley Street. The sculpture was

made by singer Tommy Steele and presented to Liverpool for the nominal sum of half a sixpence.

8 *The International Garden Festival* The greatest show in the world during 1984 and the biggest exhibition in the UK this century since the Festival of Britain. Opened by the Queen in May 1984, the show had a special Beatles' waterfall display with a genuine yellow submarine.

9 *The Jacaranda Club* The original club was sold in the mid-sixties and turned into a steak bar. For the Liverpool '84 celebrations, the old name was revived and the Slater Street venue, when undergoing redecoration, was found to have uncovered some of Stu Stucliffe's murals in the basement.

10 *The Walker Art Gallery* Magnificent gallery in William Brown Street, one of the best in the UK. In May 1984, a special 'Art Of The Beatles' exhibition was launched there. This was the gallery which held the annual John Moore's Exhibitions in which Stu Sutcliffe sold a painting, bought a guitar and became a Beatle!

96 An Orchard Of Apples

The Beatles intended Apple Records to be a launching pad for new artists, in addition to their own releases. The label was launched in 1968 and it did, indeed, discover a number of excellent artists. The Apple records issued in the UK were:

SINGLES

Hey Jude c/w *Revolution* The Beatles (30th August 1968)
Those Were The Days c/w *Turn Turn Turn* Mary Hopkin (30th August 1968)
Sour Milk Sea c/w *The Eagle Laughs At You* Jackie Lomax (6th September 1968)
Thingumybob c/w *Yellow Submarine* The Black Dyke Mills Band (6th September 1968)
Maybe Tomorrow c/w *And Her Daddy's A Millionaire* The Iveys (15th November 1968)
Road To Nowhere c/w *Illusions* Trash (24th January 1969)
Goodbye c/w *Sparrow* Mary Hopkin (28th March 1969)

Get Back c/w *Don't Let Me Down* (11th April 1969)

New Day c/w *Fall Inside Your Eyes* Jackie Lomax (9th May 1969)

The Ballad of John and Yoko c/w *Old Brown Shoe* (30th May 1969)

That's The Way God Planned It c/w *What About You* Billy Preston (27th June 1969)

Give Peace A Chance c/w *Remember Love* The Plastic One Band (4th July 1969)

Walls Ice Cream, special promotional single, made in conjunction with a publicity campaign by the ice-cream manufacturers.

Hare Krishna Mantra c/w *Prayer To The Spiritual Master* Radha Krishna Temple (29th August 1969)

Golden Slumbers c/w *Carry That Weight* Trash (3rd October 1969)

Give Peace A Chance c/w *Living Without Tomorrow* The Hot Chocolate Band (10th October 1969)

Everything's Alright c/w *I Want To Thank You* Billy Preston (17th October 1969)

Cold Turkey c/w *Don't Worry Kyoko* The Plastic Ono Band (24th October 1969)

Something c/w *Come Together* The Beatles (31st October 1969)

Come And Get It c/w *Rock Of All Ages* Badfinger (5th December 1969)

Temma Harbour c/w *Lontano Dagli Occhi* Mary Hopkin (16th January 1970)

All That I've Got c/w *As I Get Older* Billy Preston (30th January 1970)

How The Web Was Woven c/w *Thumbin' A Ride* Jackie Lomax (6th February, 1970)

Ain't That Cute c/w *Vaya Con Dios* Doris Troy (13th February 1970).

Instant Karma c/w *Who Has Seen The Wind* John/Yoko With The Plastic Ono Band (20th February 1970)

Govinda c/w *Govinda Jai Jai* Radha Krishna Temple (6th March 1970)

Let It Be c/w *You Know My Name* The Beatles (6th March 1970)

Knock Knock Who's There c/w *I'm Going To Fall In Love Again* Mary Hopkin (20th March 1970)

Jacob's Ladder c/w *Get Back* Doris Troy (28th August 1970)

Think About Your Children c/w *Heritage* Mary Hopkin (16th October 1970)

No Matter What c/w *Better Days* Badfinger (6th November 1970)

Carolina In My Mind c/w *Something's Wrong* James Taylor (6th November 1970)

My Sweet Lord c/w *What Is Life* George Harrison (15th January 1971)

Another Day c/w *Oh Woman Oh Why* Paul McCartney (19th February 1971)

Power To The People c/w *Open Your Box* John Lennon and The Plastic Ono Band (12th March 1971)

It Don't Come Easy c/w *Early 1970* Ringo Starr (9th April 1971)

Try Some Buy Some c/w *Tandoori Chicken* Ronnie Spector (16th April 1971)

Let My Name Be Sorrow c/w *Kew Gardens* Mary Hopkin (18th June 1971)

God Save Us c/w *Do The Oz* Bill Elliott And The Elastic Oz Band (16th July 1971)

Bangla Desh c/w *Deep Blue* George Harrison (30th July 1971)

Back Seat Of My Car c/w *Heart Of The Country* Paul and Linda McCartney (13th August 1971)

Joi Bangla/Oh Bhaugowan c/w *Raga Mishri Jhinjhoti* Ravi Shankar (27th August 1971)

Mrs. Lennon c/w *Midsummer New York* Yoko Ono (29th October 1971)

Water Paper And Clay c/w *Hefferson* Mary Hopkin (3rd December 1971)

Day After Day c/w *Sweet Tuesday Morning* Badfinger (14th January 1972)

Mind Train c/w *Listen The Snow Is Falling* Yoko Ono (21st January 1972)

Give Ireland Back To The Irish c/w *Give Ireland Back To The Irish* Wings (25th February 1972)

Back Off Boogaloo c/w *Blindman* Ringo Starr (17th March 1972)

Mary Had A Little Lamb c/w *Little Woman Love* Wings (12th May 1972)

We're On Our Way c/w *Supersoul* Chris Hodge (1st June 1972)

Saturday Night Special c/w *Valse De Soleil Coucher* Sundown Playboys (24th November 1972)

Happy Xmas (War Is Over) c/w *Listen The Snow Is Falling* John/Yoko And The Plastic Ono Band (24th November 1972)

Hi Hi Hi c/w *C Moon* Wings (1st December 1972)

Power Boogie c/w *Liberation Special* Elephant's Memory (8th December 1972)

Warm Woman c/w *More Than Words* Lon and Derrek Van Eaton (9th March 1973)

My Love c/w *The Mess* Paul McCartney And Wings (23rd March 1973)

Death of Samantha c/w *Yang Yang* Yoko Ono (4th May 1973)

Give Me Love (Give Me Peace On Earth) c/w *Miss O'Dell George Harrison (25th May 1973)*

Live And Let Die c/w *Lie Around* Wings (1st June 1973)

Photograph c/w *Down And Out* Ringo Starr (19th October 1973)

Helen Wheels c/w *Country Dreamer* Paul McCartney And Wings (26th October 1973)

Run Run Run c/w *Men Men Men* Yoko Ono (9th November) 1973)

Mind Games c/w *Meat City* John Lennon (16th November 1973)

You're Sixteen c/w *Devil Woman* Ringo Starr (8th February 1974)

Jet c/w *Let Me Roll It* Paul McCartney And Wings (15th February 1974)

Apple Of My Eye c/w *Blind Owl* Badfinger (8th March 1974)

Band On The Run c/w *Zoo Gang* Paul McCartney And Wings (28th June 1974)

Whatever Gets You Thru The Night c/w *Beef Jerky* John Lennon (4th October 1974)

Junior's Farm c/w *Sally G* Paul McCartney And Wings (25th November 1974)

Only You c/w *Call Me* Ringo Starr (15th November 1974)

Ding Dong c/w *Don't Care Anymore* George Harrison (6th December 1974)

Number 9 Dream c/w *That You Got* John Lennon (31st January 1975)

Sally G c/w *Junior's Farm* Paul McCartney and Wings (7th February 1975)

Snookeroo c/w *Oo-Wee* Ringo Starr (21st Feburary 1975)

Dark Horse c/w *Hari's On Tour* George Harrison (28th February 1975)

Stand By Me c/w *Move Over Ms. L.* John Lennon (18th April 1975)

You c/w *World Of Stone* George Harrison (12th September 1975)

Imagine c/w *Working Class Hero* John Lennon (24th October 1975)

Oh My My c/w *No No Song* Ringo Starr (9th January 1976)

This Guitar (Can't Keep From Crying) c/w *Maya Love* George Harrison (6th February 1976)

Hey Jude c/w *Revolution* The Beatles (6th March 1976)

Get Back c/w *Don't Let Me Down* The Beatles (6th March 1976)

The Ballad Of John And Yoko c/w *Old Brown Shoe* The Beatles (6th March 1976)

Something c/w *Come Together* The Beatles (6th March 1976)

Let It Be c/w *You Know My Name* The Beatles (6th March 1976)

My Sweet Lord c/w *What Is Life* George Harrison (20th November 1976)

Hey Jude c/w *Revolution* The Beatles (3rd December 1982)

Get Back c/w *Don't Let Me Down* The Beatles (3rd December 1982)

The Ballad Of John And Yoko c/w *Old Brown Shoe* The Beatles (3rd December 1982)

Something c/w *Come Together* The Beatles (3rd December 1982)

Let It Be c/w *You Know My Name* The Beatles (3rd December 1982)

ALBUMS

Wonderwall Music George Harrison (1st November 1968)

The Beatles The Beatles (22nd November 1968)

Unfinished Music No. 1 – Two Virgins John And Yoko (29th November 1968)

James Taylor James Taylor (6th December 1968)

Under The Jasmine Tree The Modern Jazz Quartet (6th December 1968)

Yellow Submarine The Beatles (17th January 1969)

Postcard Mary Hopkin (21st February 1969)

Is This What You Want Jackie Lomax (21st March 1969)

Unfinished Music No. 2 – Life With The Lions John And Yoko (9th May 1969)

Electronic Sound George Harrison (9th May 1969)

That's The Way God Planned It Billy Preston (22nd August 1969)

Abbey Road The Beatles (26th September 1969)

Space The Modern Jazz Quartet (24th October 1969)

The Wedding Album John And Yoko (7th November 1969)

Plastic Ono Band – Live Peace in Toronto 1969 The Plastic Ono Band (12th December 1969)

Magic Christian Badfinger (9th January 1970)

Sentimental Journey Ringo Starr (27th March 1970)

McCartney Paul McCartney (17th April 1970)

Let It Be The Beatles (8th May 1970)

Doris Troy Doris Troy (11th September 1970)

Encouraging Words Billy Preston (11th September 1970)

The Whale John Tavener (25th September 1970)

Beaucoups Of Blues Ringo Starr (25th September 1970)

Let It Be The Beatles (6th November 1970)

No Dice Badfinger (27th November 1970)

All Things Must Pass George Harrison (30th November 1970)

John Lennon Plastic Ono Band John Lennon And The Plastic Ono Band (11th December 1970)

Yoko Ono Plastic Ono Band Yoko Ono And The Plastic Ono Band (11th December 1970)

From Them To Us The Beatles (18th December 1970)

Radha Krishna Temple Radha Krishna Temple (28th May 1971)

Ram Paul And Linda McCartney (28th May 1971)

James Taylor James Taylor (25th June 1971)

Celtic Requiem John Tavener (2nd July 1971)

Earth Song – Ocean Song Mary Hopkin (1st October 1971)

Imagine John Lennon (8th October 1971)

Fly Yoko Ono (3rd December 1971)

Wild Life Wings (7th December 1971)

The Concert For Bangla Desh Various Artists (10th January 1972)

Straight Up Badfinger (11th February 1972)

Imagine John Lennon (June 1972)

Sometime In New York City John And Yoko (15th September 1972)

Elephant's Memory Elephant's Memory (10th November 1972)

Those Were The Days Mary Hopkin (24th November 1972)

Phil Spector's Christmas Album Various Artists (8th December 1972)

Brother Lon And Derrek Van Eaton (9th February 1973)

Approximately Infinite Universe Yoko Ono 16th February 1973)

In Concert 1972 Ravi Shankar (13th April 1973)

The Beatles 1962–1966 The Beatles (20th April 1973)

The Beatles 1967–1970 The Beatles (20th April 1973)

Red Rose Speedway Paul McCartney And Wings (4th May 1973)

Living In The Material World George Harrison (22nd June 1973)

Ringo Ringo Starr (9th November 1973)

Mind Games John Lennon (16th November 1973)

Feeling The Space Yoko Ono (23rd November 1973)

Band On The Run Paul McCartney And Wings (7th December 1973)

Ass Badfinger (8th March 1974)

Walls And Bridges John Lennon (4th October 1974)

Goodnight Vienna Ringo Starr (15th November 1974)

Dark Horse George Harrison (20th December 1974)

Rock 'n' Roll John Lennon (21st February 1975)

Extra Texture (Read All About It) George Harrison (3rd October 1975)

Shaved Fish (Collectable Lennon) John Lennon (24th October 1975)

Blast From Your Past Ringo Starr (12th December 1975)
The Beatles 1962–1966 The Beatles (November 1978)
The Beatles 1967–1970 The Beatles (November 1978)
The Beatles The Beatles (1979)
Let It Be The Beatles (1979)

97 The Best Of Cellars

The Cavern Club in Mathew Street, Liverpool, became the
most famous club of the sixties. On 26th April 1984, a new
Cavern Club was opened on the exact site of the original. Here
are some facts about the club where the Beatles made so many
appearances:

The club was the brainchild of Alan Sytner, a Liverpool doctor's son. His inspiration came from a Parisian Jazz cellar called
Le Caveau.

The club officially opened at 7.20 pm on 16th January 1957,
20 minutes later than advertised.

There were over 2,000 people queueing up for entrance on
the first night, but only 600 managed to get in.

One of the first acts on stage on opening night was a local
outfit, the Coney Island Skiffle Group – the Club was due to be
opened by the Earl of Wharncliffe, but he couldn't make it.

Ringo Starr appeared there with a group called The Darktown Skiffle Group

Ray McFall, accountant for the Sytner family, took over the
club from Alan in October 1959.

Initially, rock music was banned at the Cavern and Rory
Storm & The Hurricanes (with Ringo on drums) were fined for
playing *Whole Lotta Shakin'*.

Due to falling business for jazz bands and skiffle groups, Ray
began to introduce regular Wednesday evening rock and roll
sessions with local bands in May 1960.

The Beatles first appeared there on Tuesday, 21st March
1961 on 'The Swinging Blue Jeans Guest Night'.

A special 'Welcome Home' night was held for the Beatles on
20th July 1961.

The Beatles were frozen in time when a Granada TV team filmed them performing *Some Other Guy* on the Cavern stage.

The group began their own regular guest nights, acting as hosts to other bands, on 2nd August 1961.

Bill Harry arranged for Brian Epstein to visit the Cavern on 9th November 1961, where he saw the Beatles for the first time

Prior to a Hamburg trip, their local fan club organised 'An Evening With John, George, Paul and Pete' on 5th April 1962.

Pete Best made his final appearance as drummer with the Beatles on 17th August 1962 at the Cavern and Ringo made his debut appearance the next night. During the scuffles with fans chanting for Pete, George received a black eye. Later that evening, Granada TV filmed the group performing *Some Other Guy*.

Brian Epstein brought George Martin to see the group at the club on 12th December 1962. The Beatles made their last Cavern appearance on 3rd August 1963 on a bill with the Escorts, the Merseybeats, the Roadrunners, the Sapphires and Johnny Ringo & The Colts.

The Cavern's resident compere, Bob Wooler, checked the club's records and announced that the Beatles had appeared there for 292 performances.

Ray McFall extended the Cavern premises by buying the cellar next door on 3rd November 1963.

When extending the premises, Ray had the original Cavern stage cut up into pieces of 'Beatleboard' which were sold at 5 shillings a piece, with proceeds donated to Oxfam.

Sunday Night At The Cavern was the name of a regular Radio Luxembourg show broadcast weekly from the club from 15th March 1963 with Bob Wooler as the host.

There was a special 'Caverncade' parading through the city on Saturday 12th September 1964, with proceeds going to Oxfam.

A recording studio, Cavern Sound, was opened on the club premises on 15th October 1964.

1st February 1964 saw the launch of a Junior Cavern Club in which under-sixteens had their own sessions each Saturday afternoon.

There was a Liverpool group called The Caverners.

In 1964, the club launched Cavern Artists Ltd, which managed and acted as agent for a number of local acts, including Earl Preston's Realms' the Hideaways, the St. Louis Checks, the Excelles, the Kubas, the Notions, the Clayton Squares and the Michael Allen Group.

The club was forced to close on 28th February 1966 with debts of £10,000. Fans, led by Beatles' fan-club secretary, Freda Kelly, barricaded themselves in the club against the bailiffs, while the Hideaways continued to perform on stage.

The third owner of the Cavern was Joe Davey, former proprieter of Joe's Café where the Beatles used to have late night meals.

The club was re-opened on 23rd July 1966 by Harold Wilson

The fourth owner of the Cavern was Roy Adams.

The club closed for the last time in 1973, when it was demolished to make way for the air vent of an underground railway station.

Beatles PR man, Tony Barrow, wrote the text for a magazine on the club which was reprinted in 1984 for sale at the club.

Cavern doorman, Pat Delaney, who worked at the club longer than any other person, was re-employed in the new premises and has been writing a book about the club called *The Best Of Cellars*.

The new Cavern was rebuilt with bricks from the original in a

£9,000,000 complex designed by architect David Backhouse.

Three local businessmen, George Downey, Stuart Granger and Tommy Smith, run the new club as Cavern Entertainments Ltd.

The new club has been built parallel to Mathew Street instead of at right angles to it, as was the original.

Inside the new club, there is a reconstruction of a Liverpool street scene and a NEMS record shop, together with a pub.

Cavern Beat is a special Beatles' film made by Abbey Road Studios for exclusive screening twice daily at the new club.

Tribute To The Cavern is a special sixteen-track album from EMI Records, also for exclusive sale at the new club.

In April 1984, the Cavern reopened with a genuine Mersey Beat bill featuring the Swinging Blue Jeans, The Merseybeats and Billy J. Kramer.

98 Things We Said Today

There are literally scores of bootleg albums containing interviews with the Beatles taken from various radio and television shows. However, interest in recorded Beatles' interviews began in 1964 with *Hear The Beatles Tell All* and continued into 1983 with *Heartplay – An Unfinished Dialogue*. Here are some of the interview albums which have been released to the general public over the years:

Hear The Beatles Tell All Originally issued in the USA in September 1964 on Vee Jay PRO 202, it contains interviews with all four members of the group, conducted by Dave Hull, and a John Lennon interview, conducted by Jim Steck. The album was issued in the UK on Charly Records CRV 202 in March 1981.

The Beatles Story A double album compilation issued on Capitol STHO 2222 on 23rd November 1964. *The Beatles Story* contained both interviews and fragments of Beatles' songs and entered the American charts.

The American Tour With Ed Rudy Issued by Radio Pulsebeat News Documentary No. 2, on June 9th 1964, this was also a chart entry. Rudy travelled with the Beatles on their 1964 tour of the USA and presented excerpts from his interviews on this album.

Ed Rudy With New U.S. Tour Second Rudy album issued on Radio Pulsebeat News L-1001/1002 in 1965. recorded during the Beatles' second tour of the USA in 1964, it contained comments from their press conferences. It didn't fare as well as the first and was not a chart hit.

The Beatles Tapes This album was issued in the UK on Polydor 2683 068 on 30th July 1976. Its full title was *The Beatles Tapes From The David Wigg Interviews* and comprised interviews conducted with the Beatles by London journalist David Wigg between the years 1968 and 1973.

Beatle Talk Issued by Great Northwest Music Co. GWC-4007 on 15th November 1978. Released more than a decade after the original recordings, the album contained excerpts from interviews by Red Robinson during Beatles' press conferences in Vancouver in August 1964 and Seattle in August 1966.

The McCartney Interview Edited from a lengthy interview with Paul conducted by Vic Garbarini for *Musician: Player And Listener* magazine. Issued on Parlophone CHAT I for one day only on 23rd February 1981 and immediately became a collectors' item.

Heartplay – An Unfinished Dialogue Issued in the UK on Polydor 817238–1 on 16th December 1983. The album contains excerpts from the twenty-two hours of taped conversations which journalist David Sheff had with John and Yoko for the *Playboy* interview, originally published in January 1981 and resurfacing as the book *The* Playboy *Interviews With John Lennon And Yoko Ono*.

99 Into The Seventies

How did the Beatles and the solo recordings of the ex-members fare in the British best-selling record lists of the seventies? Year by year, the best-sellers of the previous 12 months were totted up – and, throughout the decade, there was always a placing for the Beatles or the individual members.

In 1970, *Let It Be* was the 46th most popular single and *Let It Be* the 3rd most popular album, with *McCartney* as the 5th most popular seller of the year with *Abbey Road* at No. 15. The following year George Harrison's *My Sweet Lord* was the most popular single, with Paul's *Another Day* at No. 25 and Ringo's *It Don't Come Easy* at No. 42. Albumwise, Paul and Linda were No. 10 in the best-sellers of the year with *Ram* and John's *Imagine* was No. 15.

In 1972, only one ex-Beatle featured in the year's lists; Ringo at No. 61 with *Back Off Boogaloo* and with *Imagine* at No. 21 in the album best-seller list. 1973 saw Paul And Wings with *Live And Let Die* at No. 75 in the list and Ringo Starr at No. 95 with *Photograph*. Ringo Starr led the list in 1974 with *You're Sixteen* at No. 28, and *Band On The Run* provided Paul And Wings with the 50th best-selling single of the year, while their *Jet* came in at No. 62. *Band On The Run* was far more successful as an album, giving Wings the No. 2 position. *The Beatles 1966–1970* was No. 23, *The Beatles 1962–1966* was No. 33 and *Sgt. Pepper's Lonely Hearts Club Band* was No. 62.

In 1975, *Imagine* at No. 83 was the only single from an ex-member of the Fab Four, although Wings fared better in the album charts at No. 9 with *Venus & Mars* while *Band On The Run* also made No. 24, with *Rock 'n' Roll* by John Lennon at No. 48, *The Beatles 1962–1966* at No. 67, *The Beatles 1967–1970* at No. 73, John's *Shaved Fish* at No. 89 and *Sgt. Pepper* at No. 93.

In 1976, Wings reached No. 23 with *Silly Love Songs* and also provided the 29th best-seller of the year with *Let 'Em In*. It was also encouraging for Wings to be in the album top-sellers with *Wings At The Speed Of Sound* at No. 4. *Band On The Run* also made the best-seller list, appearing at No. 74 with *The Beatles 1962–1966* at No. 76 and *The Beatles 1967–1970* at No. 80; *Rock And Roll Music* by the Beatles also clocked in at No. 94.

1977 was the year of Britain's all-time best-selling single, *Mull Of Kintyre*, safely settled as the No. 1 best-seller. In the album charts, *The Beatles At The Hollywood Bowl* was No. 29 and *Wings Over America* No. 48. *Mull Of Kintyre* still had an effect on the 1978 best-sellers, entering in the position of No.

22, while, in the album charts, Wings were at No. 29 with *London Town* and *The Beatles Love Songs* appeared at No. 70.

1979 saw *Goodnight Tonight* by Wings at No. 73 in the singles' best-seller list with *Wings Greatest* at No. 43 in the album best-sellers and *Back To The Egg* by Wings at No. 74.

100 Sing A Song Of Beatles

Since 1964, when the Beatles made their first impact on the USA, musicians of all persuasions have found the Lennon & McCartney songs open to interpretation in a number of styles, ranging from jazz to classical. There have been interpretations in a baroque music style, by banjo, by harmonica, in the big band and even the country music style. *Singalong With The Beatles* is a purely instrumental interpretation of their numbers, of which Liverpool's eccentric Fritz Spiegl produced an inimitable version in a classical manner. Artists ranging from Count Basie to the Boston Pops Orchestra have devoted complete albums to the music of the Beatles and the Hollyridge Strings produced a series of five instrumental albums of Beatles' music. There have been many other interpretations from acts such as The Brothers Four and Mary Wells (*Love Songs To The Beatles*) and the following list is just a selection of such numbers:

Off The Beatle Track
The George Martin Orchestra. Issued in the UK on 10th July 1964, on Parlophone PCS 3057, and in the USA on United Artists UAS 6377 on 3rd August. Tracks: *All My Loving; Don't Bother Me; Can't Buy Me Love; All I've Got To Do; I Saw Her Standing There; She Loves You; From Me To You; There's A Place; This Boy; Please Please Me; Little Child; I Want To Hold Your Hand.*

Harmonica Beatlemania
Billy Lee Riley. Issued in the USA in 1964 on Mercury 20974. Tracks: *Love Me Do; I'll Cry Instead; A Hard Day's Night; Can't Buy Me Love; She Loves You; I Saw Her Standing There; Please Please Me; Tell Me Why; All My Loving; I Should Have Known Better; Ringo's Theme.*

210

A Royal occasion for Paul and Linda when they attended the Philharmonic Orchestra's performance at the Royal Albert Hall, which was attended by Her Majesty the Queen and His Royal Highness The Duke of Edinburgh. Paul was given a standing ovation when he was spotted in his box.

George Martin's long association with the Beatles was to result in him recording most of their major hits with his own orchestra.

The Beatles Greatest Hits

Santo And Johnny. Issued in North America in 1964 on Canadian American 1017. Tracks: *A Hard Day's Night; Do You Want To Know A Secret?; She Loves You; I Want To Hold Your Hand; The Beatle Blues; I Saw Her Standing There; And I Love Her; All My Loving; P.S. I Love You; Please Please Me; The Beatle Stomp; Can't Buy Me Love.*

Singalong With The Beatles – Instrumental Backgrounds

Issued in the USA in 1965 on Tower 5000. Tracks: *A Hard Day's Night; I Saw Her Standing There; Love Me Do; She Loves You; Please Please Me; She's A Woman; I Feel Fine; P.S. I Love You; Can't Buy Me Love; All My Loving; I Want To Hold Your Hand.*

The Chipmunks Sing The Beatles Hits

Issued in the USA on Liberty LST 7388 in 1964 and in the UK in 1965 on Liberty LBY 1218. Tracks: *All My Loving; Do You Want To Know A Secret?; She Loves You; From Me To You; Twist And Shout; A Hard Day's Night; P.S. I Love You; Michelle; I'll Follow The Sun; Can't Buy Me Love; I'll Cry Instead; And I Love Her; She's A Woman; If I Fell; Things We Said Today.*

The Baroque Beatles Book

Joshua Rifkin. Issued in the USA in 1965 on Elektra 7306. Tracks: *I Want To Hold Your Hand; I'll Cry Instead; Things We Said Today; You've Got To Hide Your Love Away; Please Please Me; Help!; Eight Days A Week; She Loves You; Thank You Girl; A Hard Day's Night.*

Eine Kleine Beatlemusik

Fritz Spiegl. Issued in the UK on 1st October 1965 on HMV 7EG 8887. Tracks: *She Loves You; A Hard Day's Night; All My Loving; Please Please Me; I Want To Hold Your Hand; I'll Get You.*

The Beatle Cracker Suite

Fritz Spiegl Issued a few weeks later on 29th October. Tracks: *It's For You; Help!; She Loves You; From Me To You; Ticket To Ride; All My Loving.*

Chet Atkins Picks On The Beatles

Issued in the USA on RCA Victor LSP 3531 in 1966. Tracks: *Yesterday; A Hard Day's Night; I Feel Fine; She Loves You;*

Michelle; I'll Follow The Sun; Can't Buy Me Love; I'll Cry Instead; And I Love Her; She's A Woman; If I Fell; Things We Said Today.

Happy Banjos Play The Beatles

The Big Ben Banjo Band. Issued in the USA on Capitol 2642 in 1967. Tracks: *All My Loving; She's A Woman; You Can't Do That; Paperback Writer; Eight Days A Week; I'll Get You; World Without Love; Any Time At All; And I Love Her; Ticket To Ride; I'm Happy Just To Dance With You; Things We Said Today; I Should Have Known Better; I'm A Loser; It Won't Be Long; A Hard Day's Night; I Feel Fine; Can't Buy Me Love; Michelle; This Boy; Yesterday; Norwegian Wood; Rain; Nowhere Man; Don't Bother Me; No Reply; Little Child; Tell Me Why; The Word; I'll Be Back.*

Francois Glorieux Plays The Beatles

Issued in the USA on Vanguard VSD 79417 in 1978. Tracks: *Yesterday; Help!; Let It Be; Can't Buy Me Love; Ob-La-Di Ob-La-Da; Hey Jude; Michelle; Yellow Submarine; Girl; Norwegian Wood; The Fool On The Hill; In My Life; Eleanor Rigby.*

Songs Of The Beatles

Sarah Vaughan. Issued in the USA on Atlantic SD 16037 in 1980. Tracks: *Get Back; And I Love Her; Eleanor Rigby; Fool On The Hill; You Never Give Me Your Money; Come Together; I Want You (She's So Heavy); Blackbird; Something; Here There And Everywhere; The Long And Winding Road; Yesterday; Hey Jude.*

Stars On Long Play

Radio Records RR 16044, issued in 1980, this Jaap Eggermont production had one side comprising Beatles' numbers: *No Reply; I'll Be Back; Drive My Car; Do You Want To Know A Secret; We Can Work It Out; I Should Have Known Better; Nowhere Man; You're Going To Lose That Girl; Ticket To Ride; The Word; Eleanor Rigby; Every Little Thing; And Your Bird Can Sing; Get Back; Eight Days A Week; It Won't Be Long; Day Tripper; Wait; Good Day Sunshine; My Sweet Lord; Here Comes The Sun; While My Guitar Gently Weeps; Taxman; A Hard Day's Night; Things We Said Today; If I Fell; You Can't Do That; Please Please Me; I Want To Hold Your Hand.*

The Royal Philharmonic Orchestra Plays The Beatles

Issued in the UK on SRFL 1001 in 1982. Tracks: *All You Need Is Love; A Hard Day's Night; I Wanna Hold Your Hand; Here There And Everywhere; Norwegian Wood; Fool On The Hill; Beatles Medley; Imagine; Blackbird; Mull of Kintyre; Happy Xmas (War Is Over); Sgt. Pepper Medley.*

James Last Plays The Greatest Songs Of The Beatles

Issued on Polydor POLD 5119 in 1983. Tracks: *Eleanor Rigby; A Hard Day's Night; Let It Be; Penny Lane; She Loves You; Michelle; Ob-La-Di Ob-La-Da; Hey Jude; Lady Madonna; All You Need Is Love; Norwegian Wood; Yesterday.*

101 Fenno's Fab Four Films

Fenno Werkman has the largest private collection of Beatles' films in the world and his speciality is to set up unique video shows at various conventions around the world. An example is the *Cavern Mecca Weekend* at the Cavern Club, Liverpool on 28th and 29th April 1984. Fenno's programme of videos was:

A Hard Day's Night
Ed Sullivan Show. Feb. 9th, 1964
Ed Sullivan Show. Feb. 16th, 1964
Ed Sullivan Show. Feb. 23rd, 1964
Shindig. Oct. 9th, 1964
Ed Sullivan Show. Aug. 14th, 1965
Sweden, 1963: 'Drop In' show
Beatles On Dutch TV, 1964
Shea Documentary, 1965
Tokyo, 1966 (white suit)
Beatle Surprise
Let It Be (out takes)
Imagine
Magical Mystery Tour
Beatle Cartoons
Yellow Submarine
Help!
Around The Beatles

The Music Of Lennon & McCartney
16 Beatle promo films
Melbourne Concert, 1964
Paris Concert, 1965
Tokyo Concert, 1966
Beatle Surprise
Let It Be (out takes)
John & Yoko – One To One Concert
Rock Arena
Beatle Cartoons
Let It Be

102 Die Beatles Kommen

Germany was the first country outside of the UK in which the Beatles gained fans. Peter Schuster of *From Me To You*, a German fanzine, conducted a readers' poll of favourite Beatles' records every 3 months from 1978 to 1980. He has composed this list of results especially for the *Book Of Beatle Lists*.

TOP 20 SINGLES IN GERMANY
 1 *Get Back*
 2 *Hey Jude*
 3 *Help!*
 4 *Let It Be*
 5 *I Am The Walrus*
 6 *My Sweet Lord*
 7 *Yes It is*
 8 *Getting Closer*
 9 *Goodnight Tonight*
10 *Revolution*
11 *Old Siam Sir*
12 *Mull Of Kintyre*
13 *Coming Up*
14 *Here, There And Everywhere*
15 *Something*
16 *Waterfalls*
17 *Girl*

18 *Imagine*
19 *Here Comes The Sun*
20 *Wonderful Christmas Time*
21 *Yesterday*
22 *Give Peace A Chance*

TOP 15 ALBUMS IN GERMANY
1 *Abbey Road*
2 *Rubber Soul*
3 *White Album*
4 *Sgt. Pepper*
5 *Back To The Egg*
6 *Revolver*
7 *Band On The Run*
8 *Please Please Me*
9 *A Hard Day's Night*
10 *George Harrison*
11 *Let It Be*
12 *With The Beatles*
13 *Help!*
14 *All Things Must Pass*
15 *McCartney II*

103 Capital's *Hall Of Fame*

Capital Radio, London's popular commercial radio station launched their *Hall Of Fame* in 1976, a list of the one hundred most popular favourites of Capital listeners. In 1978, the *Hall Of Fame* was increased to 500 titles and in 1983, Capital Radio listeners once more voted for their 500 all-time favourite records via d.j. Roger Scott's afternoon programme. The Beatles and Beatles-related records in the 1983 *Hall Of Fame* were:

4   *Hey Jude* The Beatles
5   *Imagine* John Lennon
27 *Woman* John Lennon
42 *Yesterday* The Beatles
54 *Strawberry Fields Forever* The Beatles

57	*Lucy In The Sky With Diamonds* The Beatles
60	*Let It Be* The Beatles
78	*A Day In The Life* The Beatles
90	*Penny Lane* The Beatles
107	*The Long And Winding Road* The Beatles
111	*Silly Love Songs* Wings
124	*Eleanor Rigby* The Beatles
136	*Can't Buy Me Love* The Beatles
163	*Mull of Kintyre* Wings
174	*Love Me Do* The Beatles
183	*In My Life* The Beatles
187	*My Sweet Lord* George Harrison
201	*She Loves You* The Beatles
248	*Band On The Run* Wings
258	*Here Comes The Sun* The Beatles
273	*Ebony And Ivory* Paul McCartney & Stevie Wonder
311	*Something* The Beatles
316	*Twist & Shout* The Beatles
415	*Maybe I'm Amazed* Wings
480	*I Feel Fine* The Beatles
489	*Michelle* The Beatles
494	*All My Loving* The Beatles
495	*Still Water (Love)* The Beatles
500	*She's A Woman* The Beatles

104 Unreleased Tracks

There are a number of studio tracks recorded over the years, which, at the time of writing, have never been released. They include:

What's The News Mary Jane
Have You Heard The Word
Futting The Futz
Maisy Jones
Baby Jane
Rubber Soul
Suzie Parker

Can He Walk
How Do You Do It?
Love Of The Loved
Woman
Step Inside Love
Goodbye
That Means A Lot
I'll Keep You Satisfied
It's For You
Shirley's Wild Accordion
Jessie's Dream
Now Hear This Song Of Mine
I Lost My Little Girl
Looking Glass
Thinking Of Linking
The Years Roll Along
Winston's Walk
Keep Looking That Way
Hello Little Girl
I'll Be On My Way
Tell Me If You Can
Shout
I Do Like To Be Beside The Seaside
If You've Got Troubles
Pink Litmus Paper Shirt
Colliding Circles
Not Unknown
Anything
India
Annie
Peace Of Mind
Those Were The Days
Not Guilty
Penina
I Should Like To Live Up A Tree
When I Come To Town
Four Nights In Moscow
You've Got To Stay With Me
Every Song Is Sung

Gotta Sing, Gotta Dance
Oriental Nightfish
My Carnival

105 McCartney's Menu

The Atlantic Hotel in Chapel Street, Liverpool, opened a unique wine bar in 1982 called *McCartney's*. The bistro has the right ambience for Beatle fans, with its selection of Beatles' records decorating the walls and tables featuring photographs and articles on the group. Of unusual interest is the bistro menu. The prices quoted are those which were current in the Summer of 1983.

COME TOGETHER SOUP
Soup of the day.   65p

PRAWN COCKTAIL
Prawns in marie-rose sauce.   £1.45p

PENNY LANE SALAD
Sliced pineapple and oranges together
with cottage cheese, served on a bed of lettuce.   90p

AVOCADO CREOLE
Avocado with prawn and pineapple
in whipped cream.   £1.80p

McCARTNEY'S MUSHROOMS
Mushrooms fried with peppers and garlic.   £1.10p

ELEANOR RIGBY SALAD
Crabmeat in marie-rose sauce, garnished with
sliced avocado, served on a bed of lettuce.   £1.75p

WHITEBAIT
Delicious fresh fried whitebait.   £1.40p

CORN-ON-THE-COB
The Transatlantic treat.   £1.35p

YELLOW MELON SUBMARINE
Refreshingly juicy.   £1.10p

OCTOPUS' GARDEN PLATTER
Mixed seafood selection served with brown bread,
tomato, cucumber, lettuce and lemon.   £1.85p

PLAICE TARTARE
A tasty, golden delight.   £2.75p

I AM THE EGG, MAN
A choice of omelettes with a variety
of favourite fillings.   £1.90p

CHEESEBOARD
Your selection of English and Continental cheeses.   85p

FRESH COFFEE
Per cup.   50p

COFFEE COCKTAILS
Fresh coffee with your choice of liqueurs
or spirits added, topped with cream.   From £1.25p

BARBEQUED SPARE RIBS
A sensational starter dish.   £1.65p

SGT. PEPPER'S STEAK
A sirloin steak served with pepper sauce.   £4.95p

McCARTNEY'S FARMHOUSE GRILL
Fried sausage, bacon, egg, black pudding,
mushrooms, tomato and fried bread.   £2.45p

GRILLED GAMMON
Served with fried eggs or grilled
pineapple rings.   £2.95p

CHICKEN KIEV
We go back to the USSR with this one.
Chicken breast, deep fried and filled with garlic but-
ter.   £4.70p

CAVERN CLUB CHICKEN
Deep fried chicken breast served with

High jinks at the Atlantic Tower as the restaurant manager Toni Antonelli and crew take the stage in *Sgt. Pepper* style.

tomato, mushrooms, bacon and
pineapple ring.   £4.35p

TWIST AND SHOUT KEBAB
Prime pieces of meat cooked on a skewer
with peppers and onions, served with
chilli or barbeque sauce.   £4.45p

BEEF BASQUAISE
Prime pieces of beef in a burgundy sauce,
with mushrooms, bacon, garlic and croutons.   £4.70p

All main course dishes include in the price french fries and
one vegetable-of-the-day or side salad. (Side salad can be
ordered as an extra item at 65p.)

CHEF'S SPECIAL
Varying daily according to our Chef's choice, see the Black-
board for details.

GRILLED STEAKS
(Approx. raw weight 8ozs.)

221

Rump or sirloin, grilled to your taste.
(Other steaks are available on request.)   £4.85p

FAB FOUR BEEFBURGERS
A choice of four different ways of serving this favourite.
Plain £2.25. With cheese £2.60. With chilli £2.30.
With egg   £2.75p

ICE CREAM SPECIALITIES
You can add a magic touch to each of these by the addition of
a liqueur, at an extra charge. See our suggestions.

BEATLE DELIGHT
This confection is a subtle selection of pineapple and banana
pieces topped with lemon sorbet, decorated with red cherries
and whipped cream.
(Suggested liqueur: Kirsch).   £1.95p

STRAWBERRY FIELDS
Strawberry ice served with fresh strawberries,
decorated with cream and cherries.
(Suggested liqueurs: Curaçao or Grand Marnier).   £1.25p

COUPE ANYTHING GOES
This sundae of mixed fruit salad is
topped with vanilla, chocolate and
strawberry ice creams.   £1.10p

DOUBLE FANTASY
Black cherries topped with vanilla ice cream
and decorated with cream and red cherries.   £1.10p

All prices are inclusive of VAT. Gratuities at customer's dis-
cretion.

106 All Aboard: The Magical
Mystery Tour

The original coach used in the Beatles' telemovie *Magical Mystery Tour* was purchased by Beatle City and restored to look
exactly as it did when the Fab Four's film was made. The Liver-

The Magical Mystery Tour bus in its new home in Liverpool.

pool museum now promotes its own tours and thousands will have the joy of being passengers in the famous bus.

Here is a list of passengers who made the original journey in September 1967:

1 Neil Aspinall (Beatles' road manager)
2 Leslie Cavendish (hairdresser)
3 George Claydon (actor)
4 Jeni Crowley (London Area Fan Club Secretary)
5 Ivor Cutler (comedian)
6 Pauline Davis (wife of Spencer Davis, with children)
7 Spencer Davis (rock star)
8 Mal Evans (Beatles' road manager)
9 Shirley Evans (accordionist – inspiration for the unreleased *Shirley's Wild Accordion*)
10 Michael Gladden (passenger)
11 George Harrison
12 Pamela Hale (with daughter Nicola, passengers)
13 Liz Harvey (passenger)
14 Nat Jackley (actor/comedian)
15 Elizabeth & Arthur Kelly (passengers)

16 Freda Kelly (National Secretary of Official Beatle Fan Club)
17 Barbara King (Essex Area Fan Club Secretary)
18 Linda Lawson (passenger)
19 John Lennon
20 Alf Manders (coach driver)
21 Alexis Mardas (Magic Alex: Apple's electronics man)
22 Paul McCartney
23 Sylvia Nightingale (Sussex Area Fan Club Secretary)
24 Jessie Robins (actress: portray's Ringo's Aunt Jessie)
25 Derek Royce (actor: Mystery Tour courier)
26 Ringo Starr
27 Bill Wall (passenger)
28 Mandy Weet (actress: Mystery Tour hostess)
29 Maggie Wright (actress: the Lovely Starlet)